GOD@WORK

Discovering the Anointing for Business

GOD@WORK

Discovering the Anointing for Business

RICH
MARSHALL

Destiny Image® Publishers, Inc.
P.O. Box 310
Shippensburg, PA 17257-0310

ISBN 0-7684-2101-2
Library of Congress Catalog Card Number: 00-131817

For Worldwide Distribution
Printed in the U.S.A.

8 9 10 11 12 13 / 06 05 04

This book and all other Destiny Image, Revival Press, MercyPlace,
Fresh Bread, Destiny Image Fiction, and Treasure House books
are available at Christian bookstores and distributors worldwide.

For a U.S. bookstore nearest you, call **1-800-722-6774**.
For more information on foreign distributors, call **717-532-3040**.
Or reach us on the Internet:
www.destinyimage.com

Dedication

This book is dedicated to the hundreds of thousands of marketplace ministers around the world who have served the Lord in obscurity, without training and without recognition for many years. You know who you are, because God has called you. Deep within your spirit there is a passion to serve the Lord, and to serve Him with integrity, character and faith. You have been misunderstood, maligned, and ridiculed. You have been accused of seeking money more than God. You have also been accused of unfaithfulness to the call of God; some have wrongly assumed that because you did not leave the business world you did not enter into ministry.

I am thrilled to tell you that God is faithful, and the work that He has begun in you, He will bring to completion. This is a new day. The body of Christ is rediscovering the essence of God at work in the marketplace, the workplace, the home, the school—your world.

I am also thrilled to tell you that you are not alone. There is an army of marketplace ministers that God is raising up for this day. I pray that this book will be an encouragement to you and to many like you who know that God is at work.

Acknowledgments

No one has been more helpful in the writing of this book than my wife, Wilma. She has been my chief intercessor, greatest supporter, best friend, and faithful partner for 35 years of marriage. As we have prayed over the message on every page, she has faithfully focused on keeping God at the center. I deeply love and admire her, and thank God daily that He brought us together.

Our grown children and their spouses, Rich and Cece Marshall and Bill and Valerie Zurn are daily walking out the message of this book. They are actively involved in the marketplace and are making an impact for the Kingdom through their commitment to business as ministry. I am so grateful to God that He has called them to serve Him in this vital arena, and that our grandchildren will be raised in the wonderful atmosphere of marketplace ministry.

The congregation at Springs of Life Fellowship in Sunnyvale, CA, heard this message, responded to it, and believed in it enough to send us out to the world with it. I know of no church like this one, and am grateful to the pastors, staff, and leadership for their support.

Ed and Ruth Silvoso and the team at Harvest Evangelism have played a vital role in giving us a forum for presenting the message of ministry in the marketplace, in the context of reaching cities. Again I thank God for the opportunity to be a part of this team as well.

Finally, the publishers at Destiny Image have believed in this message and have faithfully seen to it that it came forth in the right time and in the right way. Thanks to Tommy Tenney for introducing us. Thanks to Don Nori, Don Milam, and Elizabeth Allen, Galen Burkholder, Sherry Cianciulli, Jeff Hall, Becky Helman, Peggy Knepper, and all of the Destiny Image family, who have helped make me an author.

Endorsements

"A dynamic new word that the Spirit is speaking to the churches these days focuses on the strategic role of marketplace ministries in the Kingdom of God. Rich Marshall has been hearing this word clearly, and thanks to his pioneer textbook, *God@Work*, you, too, can get up to speed on this incredible movement of God. This cutting-edge book needs to be in the hands of every Christian leader in our country!"

—C. Peter Wagner
Chancellor, Wagner Leadership Institute

"Rich Marshall is a pioneer among church leaders who are taking a fresh look at the marketplace. He sees that God is calling people to business and the professions with the same intensity and sense of mission as a minister is called into church work. I'm grateful that *God@Work* provides biblically based insights for what is happening. I found it a wonderful affirmation for God's business call on my life."

—John D. Beckett
President, R. W. Beckett Corporation
Author, *Loving Monday: Succeeding in Business Without Selling Your Soul*

"Rich Marshall is our friend and a pastor to pastors. As a theological entrepreneur, his teaching will help to advance the frontiers of our biblical understanding. *God@Work* will help the church to recover the other half of its evangelistic force. It will reduce the guilt and frustration caused by a misconception of what it means to be called of God. This book is practical, concrete, and immediately applicable. I encourage you not only to read it, but to study and apply it."

—Sergio Scataglini
President, Scataglini Ministries, Inc.

"Rich Marshall has not only made a convincing case that God is using businessmen and women to bring revival, he also shows us how to train and release business leaders into their calling as kings in the coming move of God. The principles in this book will help the kings and priests (church leaders) to work together to heal their broken cities."

—Dr. Jack Deere
Dean, Wagner Leadership Institute

"Still wondering what you're going to be when you grow up? How about a king or a priest? Rich Marshall renders a walloping blow, awakening a global church suffering acute identity crisis/paralysis/amnesia. He delivers the electrifying punch to vivify and to equip the kings camouflaged in blue or white collars."

—Dr. Reba Rambo-McGuire
Revivalist, Singer, Author

"Rich Marshall is trumpeting the call for those in the marketplace to see their rightful place in ministry—the workplace. *God@Work* is a much-needed call to pastors and businesspeople to understand and embrace the unique role of the marketplace in the body of Christ. It affirms God's invitation to them to see their work as a God-ordained calling."

—Os Hillman
President, Marketplace Leaders
Author, *TGIF: Today God Is First*

"Rich Marshall's book, *God@Work*, is an excellent treatise on the subject of marketplace reconciliation. It is an absolute must for all of us to expedite tearing down the wall between clergy and laity that has damaged so much of the mission of the Church. I believe strongly in the need to tear this wall down and this book is an integral part of that strategy. It is spiritually invigorating to watch men and women receive God's anointing to take the Kingdom of God to their place of work."

—Ed Silvoso
President, Harvest Evangelism

"The marketplace and the institutional Church have long been divided by barriers which need not exist. In this book, Reverend Rich Marshall utilizes the immense power of repentance, forgiveness, and spiritual awakening to bridge the historical gap and reconcile kings and priests. This book offers a road map to unity in Christ to the glory of God."

—Jay Bennett
The Kingdom Oil Company
Minneapolis, Minnesota

"In *God@Work* Rich Marshall provides a must-read for everyone who either feels, or wants to feel, the hand of God on his or her life. He shows how to look for it, how to recognize it, and how to respond faithfully to it. Excellent!"

—Thorne Auchter
(former) Adminstrator
Occupational Safety and Health Administration

"For years, I thought being in ministry meant that you had to quit your profession, enroll in seminary, and be ordained. Rich Marshall provides a solid biblical exegesis for the concept that as business executives, we are called to be in full-time ministry right where we are—in our workplaces, all day, every day. It is a must-read book for every Christian businessperson."

—C.W. Randell
President, Federal News Service
Washington, DC

"Finally...a book has been written that will release every believer into his or her true calling. The days of sitting on the bench or viewing the Kingdom from the stands are over. Rich Marshall makes it plain...we are all players on God's team."

—Dick Bernal
Senior Pastor, Jubilee Christian Center
San Jose, California

Contents

Foreword

The nation of Israel always functioned best when there were both kings and priests in place. Holy kings and spiritual priests created the synergy needed for the kingdom to move forward. One of the things that the modern Church has failed to recognize is that just as someone can be anointed to preach or sing, someone can also be *anointed for business*. The Scripture says that God "made us kings and priests" (Rev. 1:6). *God ordained the duality of dominions.* It's time for man to release what God has recognized!

Kings must worship and priests must understand business principles, but most of the time the area of their dominion specifies their area of service. Kings are anointed for business; it comes naturally and easily. Kings easily rise to the task of taking dominion in the political realm and reaping profits in the secular realm.

Priests traffic uneasily in the marketplaces of the earthly, but they can pass blindfolded through the realm of the heavenly. We honor the "priestly anointing" in our pastors, our missionaries, our worship leaders. But we must never forget that there should also be "kings." That doesn't put kings in a position higher than priests, but it does say that they are as necessary as priests.

If we are to really take back what satan has stolen from us, we must recognize the kings among us—anointed men and women who can reclaim dominion in the realm of politics and money. The church needs to validate God's anointing on them. Recognize and release what God anoints! Paul said, "But we will not boast of things without our *measure*, but according to the *measure* of the rule which God hath distributed to us (2 Cor 10:13a KJV). The Greek word there is *metron*, which means "limited portion or sphere of influence." Most people are not quite sure what their *metron*, their area of God-given influence, is, so they attempt to operate outside their giftings. The Church has been filled with the pitiful sight of people struggling outside of their sphere, truly "out of their league," and out of place like an arm out of joint. This book, *God@Work: Discovering the Anointing for Business*, is "the cure the doctor ordered" to put that arm back in place.

Thank you, Rich Marshall, for restoring the credibility of the kingly anointing. When we honor the "kings" (anointed for their sphere of influence in the earthly realm) just as we honor the "priests" (anointed for their influence in the heavenlies), then two realms combine and the rule of God begins. His will is being done "on earth as in heaven"!

"Of the increase of His government...there will be no end..."(Isa. 9:7)—neither in the earthly realm nor in the heavenlies!

—Tommy Tenney
Author, GodChaser

Chapter One

Kings and Priests

And has made us kings and priests to His God and Father, to Him be glory and dominion forever and ever. Amen (Revelation 1:6).

A new breed of ministers is emerging in the world marketplace. These ministers are passionate about the Kingdom, and are people of integrity and high moral character. They think strategically and creatively about ways to impact the world for the Lord. They are called of God and know it, but not in the traditional sense of preaching, teaching, or even evangelism as we have known it. They serve the Lord, but not in church offices or mission headquarters. They serve Him in the marketplace. Why? Because they are business and professional people, and they know that their work is their ministry.

They are called of God to make money—a lot of it. Even though they have been warned that this could greatly harm their holiness, they know that God is leading and blessing them. They are called to be creative and to think strategically about transforming their workplace, their city, and their nation. They know that God has called them to live for Christ, as lambs among wolves (see Lk. 10:3). They believe that God will use them to do miracles in the marketplace. They know that the call of God is upon them to shepherd those believers not currently attending an organized church.

This is a book of hope for a new breed of ministers. It will help the business and professional person rediscover his destiny, and will help him step into the plan that God has for his life. That destiny is your call to see the marketplace as your ministry place.

I have been a pastor for over 30 years and fully understand the drive to recruit workers for church programs. But the truth is, we will not see our nation transformed by God through this strategy. We have been trying it for years and have not seen our cities transformed. It is time to rediscover the activity of God in the world. I will tell you right now, it will not look very much like most Sunday morning congregations. I am excitedly looking forward to the day when the Body of Christ recognizes that God is spreading His servants throughout society, and that ministry is to be carried out by the entire Body of Christ. I also look forward to the time when Monday's marketplace ministry is as recognized and regular as ministry on a Sunday.

False Labels

Through the years there have been many attempts to bring about an understanding of God's calling on the entire Body of Christ. Two of the more popular and useful concepts were the phrases, *priesthood of all believers* and *every Christian a minister* which are born out of First Peter 2:9-10. From this passage we understand that all of us are called; we are a "chosen generation, a royal priesthood, a holy nation, His own special people." However, most of the time we choose to use the word *priesthood* and ignore the word *royal. Darby's Translation* uses the phrase *kingly priesthood*. I believe that Peter used both the word *priesthood* and the word *royal* or *kingly*, for the same reason that the Lord Jesus called us kings and priests (see Rev. 1:6).

Certainly there is a call to serve in the local church setting. I have personally followed that call for years. I am neither downplaying this, nor advocating that businesspeople take over local church

2

leadership and relegate the pastor to "priestly" duties. There have been cases where this has been attempted with far less than desirable results. Occasionally I will run into a godly minister who feels threatened by the idea of businesspeople in ministry. One told me he didn't want some businessman "taking over this ministry." That is not my message.

Don't confuse the call to ministry in the marketplace with the call to ministry in the local church. We need both the kings and priests ministering in their respective callings to see the national transformation we desire.

Hope for Frustated Businesspeople

I know of many who are anointed for business, yet are frustrated in that anointing because there has not been a freedom and release to operate fully in the marketplace. Some of these entrepreneurs are made to feel unspiritual when they make a lot of money, or when God prospers them in the "secular" arena. Nevertheless, I believe that day of frustration is ending, and the anointing for business will soon come into full recognition.

I certainly have no problem with using "priesthood of all believers" to lead people into an understanding of the call of God for all Christians. And I know it does help to quiet the false idea that only the "clergy" are called. However, in my own experience I have seen that the emphasis usually remains on church-related ministry. I have seen these terms used almost exclusively to recruit workers for church or mission-related endeavors. The words *priest* or *priesthood* automatically draws our thoughts to church or mission-related activities. It is my conviction that in these days, ministry must have a much broader base than church-related activities and concerns.

That is why I speak of rediscovering the original and biblical norms for business and professional people. I am quite certain that the time has come to recognize not only that all of us are called of God, but that our calling is for ministry in all facets of society. I see that calling not only in what might normally be included in the business and professional arena, but also in government,

3

sports, media, medicine, and in all areas of work life. I include all of those under the more general heading of business and professionals, or more succinctly, *kings*—people whom God has placed in positions of leadership.

Some students of Scripture have a problem with referring to Christians as "kings" and believe the word *priest* should be used exclusively.

I have no problem with that, and am not endeavoring to be particularly theological or scholarly with the use of the terms *kings* and *priests*. Rather I am trying to be practical, to use biblical terms as replacements (or at least clarifying) for the more popular and yet unbiblical terms *clergy* and *laity*.

During the years of my ministry, these were the only terms that I knew to describe the difference between pastors and Christian businesspeople. While many people, both in the Church and out of the Church, may understand the basic meanings of those terms, they do not accurately represent the heart of God. The word *laos* in Greek is the word for "the people," and that is likely the source for the word *laity* or *layman*. The word *clergy* may have its root in the Greek word *ekklesia*. That is the basis for the English word *ecclesiastic* and basically refers to the Church as the ones called out. I wonder if "clergy" did not come out of the second part of the Greek word, *klesis*, a calling, or *kaleo*, to call. That would be consistent with the misguided belief that the "clergy" are the "called" and the "laity" are the "people." But if that is the source of the word *clergy*, and I can find no other, then it is wrong in its very foundation. For *ekklesia* referred to Church in total as being the called ones. You see, I can find no biblical basis for teaching a two-class Christianity of "the people" and "the clergy."

In most cases when we used the word *clergy*, it was referring to those who had responded to a call of God in their lives and were serving Him in a "professional" capacity. Usually it would mean that they were "ordained" and drew a part, if not all, of their means of livelihood from funds derived through "professional" ministry sources. These clergy types could be pastors, missionaries, church staff, Bible teachers, theologians, leaders in a variety of

Christian organizations, or any of a number of other possibilities. But whatever the specific assignment, it was pretty clear, they were the "clergy."

"Laity," on the other hand, referred to Christians who were not in the "professional ministry," and the implication was that if they had a call from God, it was not as high a call as the one to "ministry." It did not really matter how committed they were to Christ, how much time or money they gave to Christian causes, or even how gifted they were in the gifts of the Spirit, or in ministry gifts; they were the "laity." In reality, some of these awesome servants of God were much more effective in winning the lost to Christ, in living a life of holiness and commitment to Christ, than some of the "clergy."

Usually in Christian settings, when these servants of the Lord would stand to speak, they would say, "I am 'just' a layman, but...."

Two little words, words that misrepresent God and His plan, have been used by the enemy to bring about the development of a caste system within the Body of Christ—those who are called to "professional ministry" or "full-time ministry": the "clergy"; and those who are not: the "laity." It is my conviction that all of us in the Body of Christ are called to "full-time ministry."

Shall We "Go Into the Ministry"?

When we allow this caste system to disturb our thinking, we create a problem for many who experience the strong call of God on their lives. We need both a terminology and a mindset that works to eliminate the "second-class citizen" concept in the Kingdom of God.

John Beckett is a business leader who has written an excellent book for business leaders: *Loving Monday*. In it he tells of his own journey into understanding the call of God. He writes,

"For years, I thought my involvement in business was a second-class endeavor—necessary to put bread on the table, but somehow less noble than the more sacred pursuits, like being a minister or a missionary. The clear impression was that to truly serve God, one must leave business and go into 'full-time Christian service.' I have met countless other businesspeople who feel the same way."[1]

For many dedicated Christians, when they feel the call of God on their life, they automatically assume like John Beckett did, that they need to "go into the ministry." When this call comes, a struggle follows that is often deeply troubling. In some situations, it can trigger a decision to leave a good position in their current line of work, possibly packing up the family and heading off to seminary. In some cases, a church might offer a position on staff, or perhaps another professional ministry opportunity becomes available. If those avenues are not pursued, a feeling of guilt and frustration at not following the call of God might set in.

I have been asked to counsel many of these who sought to find the will of God. Usually they open the discussion with an explanation of how they are sensing God's call, and that they need to know what to do next. The truth is, in many cases the call is very real, and it is a call from God to ministry. But it is not a call to leave their current position as much as it is to discover that God had called them into that very arena, and will therefore bless them in it, and anoint them for it. I know of dozens of people who have spent years in church work, thinking that this is what God had called them to, only to discover that they did not fit at all. The problem was not that there was no call; quite the opposite, the call was strong. It was just that it was a call to minister in the marketplace instead of the church. Others have spent those same years of guilt and frustration while in business, feeling somehow that they were not following God.

Terms to Break the Caste System

Since I understood this, and was frustrated myself at not knowing what to say and how to counsel them, I was instantly caught up with a concept I heard first from Pastor Dick Bernal at Jubilee Christian Center in San Jose, California. Our church in Sunnyvale had planned to host a conference with Dr. Jack Deere and Paul Cain. But as we watched the interest rise for this conference, we realized that our facilities were not large enough to accommodate the anticipated crowd. My wife and I felt led of the

Lord to approach Pastor Bernal about using the facilities at Jubilee. Even though the event was only a couple of weeks away, he gave us an immediate "yes."

During one of the conference sessions, Pastor Bernal used the phrase, *kings and priests*. As I heard him talk, I realized that he was calling the business and professional people "kings" and the clergy "priests." To put it mildly, he had piqued my interest. As we talked in the back room, we looked at Revelation 1:6. As I read these words, I saw for the first time a biblical way to differentiate between the callings of the professional ministry and the business and professional leaders, and at the same time, honor both of them. The words *clergy* and *laity*, of course, also differentiate between the callings, but instead of honoring, they tend to separate and isolate. The word *laity* is a demeaning word to many sincere and dedicated followers of Christ. These people know they have a call of God on their lives, and yet are subjected to a system that allows them to support ministry, especially with their money, but it does not allow them to function in ministry. So read these words from God's Word and let them penetrate your heart.

> *And from Jesus Christ, the faithful witness, the firstborn from the dead, and the ruler over the kings of the earth. To Him who loved us and washed us from our sins in His own blood, and has made us kings and priests to His God and Father, to Him be glory and dominion forever and ever. Amen* (Revelation 1:5-6).

Here in the Bible were two words that referred to "us" (see Rev. 1:6) that could be used to describe the calling of God for His Body. I am not trying to make a theological statement, rather a practical statement. Why not refer to the ones called to business and professions as "kings," and the ones called to church and mission settings as "priests"?[2] Those who are employees could choose the category of their liking. Is that exactly what the Lord had in mind when He used the words *kings* and *priests*? I doubt it. But remember I am trying to make a practical statement, using analogy, not theology. In the way that we speak of "God's generals," or "gatekeepers of the city," I am simply taking a term and applying meaning to it. I know that God has an equal call on all His servants, including those who are "just" employees. I know that He does not like the caste system that we have generated and perpetuated through the years. But I have not yet found a better or more biblical way to describe this calling.

I asked Pastor Bernal for a copy of his sermons on the topic, and this was the launching of the continued studies that have occupied much of my time since that day.

"King"—An Old Testament Term

It is interesting to note that the Lord reverts back to Old Testament language, where He uses the terms *kings* and *priests* in the passage mentioned. In the New Testament we are used to hearing terms like *pastor, teacher, evangelist, prophet, apostle, elder, deacon,* and even *priest*. All of these terms, along with *missionary*, can be gathered together under the general heading of "priest." That is, these are ministries that are very similar in nature to the ministry of the priests in the Old Testament. The New Testament does refer to priests and, as I mentioned earlier, even calls us a "royal priesthood" (see 1 Pet. 2:9). As a result we have little trouble relating to the ministry of the priest.

The word *king*, like *priest*, is an Old Testament term used to describe another of God's specially called servants. For right now, I will simply mention that the priest and/or prophet worked and ministered together with the king, but his calling was different. (Note: I will use the words *kings* and *priests* instead of the words *laity* and *clergy*, and will use *priest* to refer to the "called" ones that would, in most cases, be called clergy. *King* will refer to the "called" ones that would generally be called laity.)

We know that the phrase *kings and priests* includes all of the Body of Christ. All of us are either a king or a priest, or both. In the Church we understand the role of the priest as church ministry, missions ministry, or some related area of ministry. But the premise of this book is that all of us are called to ministry, and the kingly ministry, whether employer or employee, becomes the role of the business and professional person.

Consecrating the "Kings"

The kingly anointing could be for the schoolteacher or the government worker; it could be for business or politics; and it might take you into carpentry or the computer industry. Those in the medical community would be included under kings as well as those just starting out in pursuit of a career in some marketplace arena. The kingly anointing covers a wide spectrum of possibilities, as both CEO and minimum wage earner could be considered as kings. For the purpose of simplicity in the book, we will usually use the term *business and professional person* or some like term to refer to ones with a "kingly anointing." Oftentimes I will simply refer to these called ones as "kings."

Ladies, you need not feel left out. I believe very strongly that God will use women powerfully in His marketplace outpouring. This is the time for the women of faith to take their stand and to step into the destiny of God. I believe in the ministry of women and I honor them in their ministry gifting. I am not going to discriminate against them. Ladies, I call you "kings" as well. The Bible says, "He has called us kings and priests," so it includes both male and female. I look at it this way: If I as a man can be the "bride" of Christ, then ladies, you can be "kings." In Christ, "there is neither male nor female..." (Gal. 3:28b).

Business and professional people need to realize that receiving a call to ministry does not automatically mean leaving their current marketplace position. There is an anointing, an equipping by God, for business. When they understand that the Lord may be calling them to make that position the platform for ministry, there is a release of freedom and power for them to fulfill the call. The newfound freedom enables a free flow of God's anointing to fall, and therefore enables them to be successful in business. I use the word *anointing* in the context of Second Corinthians 1:21-22 (see also 1 Jn. 2:20,27), where we are told that it is God who anoints.

According to *Strong's Dictionary*, the word anointed means "enduing Christians with the gifts of the Holy Spirit."[3] Accompanying it are:

1. Stability—"He establishes us" and
2. The seal of the Holy Spirit—"He has sealed us and given us the Spirit in our hearts as a guarantee."

Where the anointing of God is, we feel secure in the Holy Spirit, we function with a power that is greater than we can possess on our own, and we expect and have faith for the plans of God to come to pass. This anointing is not just for church meetings. First John 2:27a tells us that "the anointing which you have received from Him abides in you." You take the anointing with you wherever you go, and therefore the anointing is powerfully available to you in the marketplace.

The business anointing allows you to make money by means of the empowerment of the Holy Spirit. It allows you to think creatively and strategically, and to receive insight directly from the Lord. The business anointing gives you that edge, that step up on the competition. It also allows you to minister in the marketplace— to pray with power, to witness and see the hand of God bring signs and wonders in your sphere of influence.

The Missing Piece

It is my conviction that the role the businessperson plays, as God works in the marketplace, is not just an important one, but may very well be the missing piece to the puzzle. I have often heard the quote: "Priests bring the vision; kings bring the provision." Let's analyze that for a moment. It is true that the priest is to bring vision. He or she is to hear from the Lord, and pass that vision on to the people of God. And it is true that kings must bring the provision. Most priests lack the funds to finance a nation-sweeping revival, and therefore I believe that it follows that one of the purposes of the kings is to bring in the funding necessary for the coming revival. But that alone is not the entire picture of the plan. The truth is that "priests" have often seen the businessperson solely as a source of funds, a deep pocket to provide resources for his vision. I have been so convicted by this attitude that the Lord often leads me to repent to the businessperson for seeing them only as a source of funds and not for the ministry gifts that are deep within them.

Is it possible for God to plant "city-reaching" and "nation-taking" strategies in the hearts of the kings? Of course it is. These kings operate in the strategic realms every day of the week. We need to open our minds to the reality that the strategies they bring to the table may not be church-related strategies, but business-related. In fact, I have seen plans to reach an entire business for Christ that are more effective in reaching lost people than some church-centered evangelistic plans. This ability to create ministry strategies; to see the destiny of God over businesses, cities, and nations; to receive vision from God; and to see God at work must not be limited to the priests. It must be released to the entire Body of Christ. I believe that when the kingly anointing falls on the Body of Christ, it will unleash a power in the Kingdom that we have not seen since the early Church.

A Kingly Warning

As we read about King David in Second Samuel 11, we find he was not doing what kings were intended to do. It was the spring of the year, and according to the Scriptures, it was time for the kings to go to war. But instead of fulfilling his assignment, his job description, the calling of God for his life, his destiny if you please, David was at home in Jerusalem.

And it was here that David got into trouble through his illicit relationship with Bathsheba. Had he gone to war like he should have, had he been concerned about fulfilling his own calling, David could have saved himself a tremendous amount of pain. Instead, David remained in Jerusalem.

And so it was that he looked from his roof to see a beautiful woman bathing. David committed adultery with Bathsheba and upon learning of her pregnancy, murdered her husband. And in David's case, it did not even end there. He also suffered the untimely death of his child and the accompanying pain he caused himself and many others.

We set ourselves up for trouble when we are out of our calling. Our hearts are susceptible to temptation when we are not doing the intended things, when we are not obeying the calling of the Lord, when we remain in bed instead of going into battle. It is at that moment, as in King David's case, that the enemy finds the opportunity to bring about a circumstance, or set of circumstances that can lead to sin, pain, and untold heartaches for ourselves and many around us, as was the case with King David.

I have seen this occur in the Body of Christ over and over again. A person receives a strong call from the Lord. The Lord is sending an anointing for powerful ministry in the business arena. However, without the understanding that the call of God may well be to stay in business, the person answers the call by entering into a priestly ministry. Now he is swimming upstream, trying to do the work of God, but without the anointing. The anointing is there, and it is a powerful anointing, but it is for "kingly ministry," not "priestly ministry." Soon frustration sets in, or possibly even his faith is affected. Maybe it is bitterness that comes—a bitterness born out of a desire to see God's blessing, while the reality is that the blessing is hidden. It is not that God does not want to bless, nor that the person is in sin. The blessings of God are being poured out, and as soon as this king realizes what his calling is—and moves into it—he puts himself in position to receive the special anointing from God.

Compounding the Problem

The problem is compounded by the use of unfortunate words by some priests. Even though in most cases no harm is intended, we priests have had a tendency to elevate the call of God on our lives so much that it appears as the highest calling. While we may not have meant it, I know that many kings have listened to pastors and heard something like this:

"I have a call of God on my life. Maybe, one day, you too can receive a call and go into the ministry like I did."

As I talk to Christian business and professional leaders today, I realize how painful these words are. Many of these godly kings are feeling put down, isolated, neglected, and confused.

I have listened on numerous occasions and, I am sorry to say, have joined in on many conversations where I and another party talked about a king who had left a priestly ministry position. In those cases I heard or used phrases like:

"And he had such a call of God on his life," or

"It's too bad he's leaving the ministry," or

"One day she'll wake up and come back."

An acquaintance of mine suffered from this kind of confusion. He was good in his priestly role and was loved by the people in his church. But he was not happy and he knew in his heart that this was not the call of God for his life. However, he had a hard time resigning his ministry. One reason involved the expectations that were put upon him from well-meaning people in the congregation. A second factor that complicated his decision to "leave the ministry" was the presence of a number of prophetic words given to him and his wife. At first glance it appeared that these prophecies could only be fulfilled in the context of church ministry. He eventually did leave his priestly position.

Recently I talked with him. He is now fulfilling his calling in the kingly role; and not only is he quite happy, but he knows he did not "leave the ministry," but rather has entered into the ministry that God destined him to fulfill. God is also blessing Him with rapid promotions and financial blessings. He can see now how those same prophetic words, words that appeared to demand he stay in his church ministry position, can surely be fulfilled in this new role. When we have only the partial understanding that all ministry is in priestly functions, we have no choice but to seek to fulfill the call in one of those functions. It is God's desire to release kings into His calling for their lives. The call of God for a king is just as real, just as powerful, just as holy, and just as righteous as His call for a priest.

Overlapping Calls

It is important to note another truth about the kingly and priestly anointing. There are some Christians who have a kingly calling with a priestly anointing. There are others who have a priestly calling with a kingly anointing. This is just another way of saying that some will cross over, that their ministry and anointing for ministry is in both kingly and priestly areas. In cases like these, I believe one calling or the other will predominate, that one of the anointings will stand out and will form the basis for the ministry. A mother is a prime example of those with dual anointing. She needs to be a priest to her children and train them in the ways of God. At the same time, she must fulfill a kingly role in running all the functions of a home.

There is no reason for us to feel that the call of God in our lives needs to be fulfilled in a priestly setting. Obviously, some are called as priests, but far more are called as kings. Both need to find a fulfilling way to meet that call. As long as the church offers her members only "church positions" for ministry, the community at large will miss out on what the Lord has designed for reaching the cities and nations. We need millions of warriors who will begin to see their job as their ministry. We need thousands of business owners who will begin to see their businesses as their ministry.

When that happens, we will have the equivalent of what happened next in the life of King David. In the case of King David, we need only wait until the next chapter to see him back on track. David went back to battle, which means he returned to what his calling as king demanded. The result was that he, and not someone else, took the city and victory was back in his hands. Even though the personal defeat he suffered through falling into temptation and sin would be dealt with (see Ps. 51), he was presently fulfilling his call. As a result, he received a great abundance of plunder from the city. David discovered that his calling was not to build the temple, but rather to finance the building of the temple. He was back on track, fulfilling his call as king.

Right now the Lord is putting many of his servants back on track. These are exciting days. Many kings are discovering the powerful calling and anointing that the Lord can give them within their own businesses.

Staying on His Path

When kings are doing kingly work, they receive a kingly anointing. The same is true with priests and the priestly anointing. In either case, the possibility of failing to fulfill the destiny of God is quite strong. But I have very good news. God is at work restoring, redeeming, and helping us to rediscover the call of God on our lives. Many are now moving into an understanding of the call of God for their lives and are starting to fulfill it. Just through my limited contacts, we are seeing an awesome display of the power of God. Many are being totally set free from their confusion. In the process, the joy of the Lord is returning in full measure, and the call of God in the lives of many kings is being released.

Gary and Kathie Williams were converted to Christ after their marriage, while they were in their early 30's. Within three years Gary felt the call of God in his life, and loaded up his family and headed off to Oklahoma to go to seminary. Gary says:

"In 1978 the Lord spoke very clearly to me concerning my going to Oral Roberts University to complete a degree in theology. I assumed that this meant a call to 'full-time ministry.' When I completed my undergraduate work, the Lord had us return to Northern California. We moved back into our home and waited for further direction. Nearly a month later I was offered a job in sales but turned it down because it was a 'secular' job.

"When a friend suggested I interview for another sales position, the Lord quickened in my spirit that this was His direction. This was very difficult for me to understand and caused a great deal of disappointment. However, out of obedience I took the job and started training. I was miserable for nearly three months until the Lord began to affirm me of my gifting. It was over a year before I understood that I was enjoying sales and had risen to be the top salesman in the nation.

"Soon the Lord had me resign my position and start my own company. My tithe grew in just a few years to be more than my annual salary had been prior to going to ORU. As the company grew, however, I still held onto the idea that there would be a day in the future when I would be able to sell the company and 'serve the Lord full time.'

"I was diagnosed with chronic fatigue syndrome in 1990 and was not given much hope for recovery. In fact, my ability to work was questionable. The Lord had us sell our home and I attempted to sell our business. Although there were several interested buyers, the Lord closed every door. As sick as I was, I continued to try to get the company through the recession that lasted for several years.

"My son and daughter joined the company and moved back to the Bay Area to come alongside me to keep the company going. Even though we enjoyed working together, we all felt that the company was a temporary assignment until we could all move on to other ways to serve the Lord. My daughter, with a Masters Degree in Social Work said she would give me only two years before she wanted to move on. As the Lord brought physical healing to me, I offered to serve in many different ways as soon as we could sell the company.

"When my Pastor was given the revelation of kings and priests, I was so relieved and excited to know that I had an anointing to do for God just what I was doing and enjoying. We have hired a woman of prayer to be part of our staff and have introduced her as a chaplain for our employees and suites tenants. What a joy to finally get it straight."

In equal proportion to the number of times that the Williams' story can be repeated, we can also repeat the story of Mark and Nancy Duarte. Today, the Duartes are happy and fulfilled in their business in Mountain View, California. They own and operate a graphic design firm that is one of the most sought after in the Silicon Valley. Major high tech companies hire them to produce their market image and some undoubtedly owe their success to the skill of Duarte Design. However, this was not always the case. In short, Mark had become a youth pastor, and had decided to go to Bible college. It was during the college years that the Lord led them to start their business. Mark and Nancy then did what many have not had the wisdom, courage, or leading to do. They left the church ministry, and entered the business ministry.

In the case of both the Williams and the Duartes, their frustration could have been erased much earlier with an understanding that when God calls an individual, He might call them to any profession, because He is Lord of them all.

Bryan Krenzin is another king who has a Bible college degree under his belt. When he graduated, he did short internships in a couple of churches, but at the same time God was leading him to start his own software design business. Bryan is a brilliant entrepreneur whom God had positioned in the Silicon Valley for His purposes. He was sincerely seeking the Lord, as were his parents, Larry and Lana, about what their role should be in bringing in the coming revival. As the messages about kings and priests were preached, they began to discover the call of God for business. According to Bryan and his parents, "We realized that the kind of work He has assigned to us is as important as that of the priest." Larry took early retirement from his corporate position, and Bryan relinquished his church internships in order to focus on the kingly business that God had placed in their hands.

I know of no family hungrier for revival. Before Wilma and I began to long and pray for revival, these folks were devouring every book on the subject, and praying daily for God to work in our society. Why then, would they step out of church-based ministry to focus on business? When Larry could retire, why did he not take a church position? The reason is they have come to understand that God can and will use them in the marketplace. God has spoken to them about strategic financing for the Kingdom, and

He has placed these committed servants in a position where the message of redemption can sound forth. These are exciting days for the business and professional person who longs for a move of God. The signs are abounding that God is about to do something big in the marketplace. Get ready! Get ready! Get ready!

Endnotes

1. John Beckett, *Loving Monday* (Downers Grove, IL: InterVarsity Press, 1998), 69.

2. Depending on the translation of the Bible that you are reading, the wording in Revelation 1:6 and 5:10 can be different.

For example, in the King James Version, The New Kings James Version, and Young's Literal Translation, the wording is "kings and priests."

In the New International Version, The New American Standard Bible, and The New Century Version, the wording is "kingdom and priests," "kingdom, priests" or "kingdom of priests."

The difference is one little Greek word, which is slightly different in the two main manuscripts used for translating the Bible. Therefore depending on which manuscript was used for the translation, you have either the singular word, which is translated "kingdom," or you have the plural word, which is translated "kings." Both of these words come from the same root word and both certainly carry the idea of royalty, or kingliness.

3. James Strong, *Strong's Exhaustive Concordance of the Bible* (Peabody, MA: Hendrickson Publishers, n.d.), **anointed** (#5548).

Chapter Two

A Life-Changing Revelation

And He said to them, "Do you not understand this parable? How then will you understand all the parables?" (Mark 4:13)

It was Christmas Sunday, and every pastor knows that you are to preach a Christmas message on that day. But my heart was stirring with a message to "kings." I had been preaching on the topic, "Kings and Priests," for three or four weeks, and had thought for sure I would be finished before Christmas, but here it was, and I could not stop.

At the same time, Mark chapter 4 was running through my mind. It is in this chapter that we read about the parable of the sower. God began to speak to my spirit out of verse 13: "Do you not understand this parable? How then will you understand all the parables?" Jesus was explaining His method of teaching. If you could understand this parable, then you could understand all the parables. If you could not understand this one, you would miss out on what He was trying to teach. Jesus was not trying to teach farmers the principles of farming, rather He was using the farming principles to teach how He operates.

When you plant a seed, whether it is wheat or the Word, you can expect a harvest. Jesus had taught about the wheat seed, but then He moved to the seed of the Word. When you sow the Word, it too produces a crop. Jesus put it like this: "But these are the ones sown on good ground, those who hear the word, accept it, and bear fruit: some thirtyfold, some sixty, and some a hundred" (Mk. 4:20). He was connecting the natural, sowing wheat seeds, with the spiritual, sowing the Word of God. What we see in the natural—the things around us, the everyday things—are lessons for us. When we begin to understand the workings of our God in the natural realm, our spiritual understanding increases.

Joseph, a Businessman

As I thought about this biblical principle, I considered my message for that Christmas Sunday. Reading in Luke chapter 1, I was struck by this idea: When God sent His Son to live on this earth, He chose to put Him in the home of a businessman. We understand that Mary is the mother of Jesus, and that God is His Father. But we also know that Joseph fulfilled the role of father on the earth. God entrusted His Son into the hands of Mary and Joseph, a carpenter—a businessman.

Later, when Wilma and I were having dinner with our friends Ray and Kay Llovio, I said, "Do you know that Jesus was born into the home of a businessman? And that if He were to be born today, God would likely put Him in the home of businessman, not the home of a pastor or missionary?" I was using the Mark 4:13 principle of understanding spiritual things in the light of natural things. I am convinced that God does nothing by mistake, and that He wastes no opportunity. Therefore, it could be that Jesus was raised in the home of a businessman as a part of the plan and purpose of God. If God had sent His Son into this society to be born of a woman, I personally believe that He would have placed Him in the home of a business leader like He did with Mary and Joseph.

Well, as soon as I said that, Kay responded, "And if John the Baptist were born today, he would be born into the home of a priest." John the Baptist's father was Zacharias, the priest.

This idea was surely going to make it into my Christmas message the next day. And so, on that Sunday morning, I was in my office praying over the message and making last-minute changes. As I prayed, I sensed the Lord speaking to me, "Do you know the impact of what you are about to say?" Well, I thought I did, but if God was asking me, obviously I did not. So I said, "No, Lord; please teach me." What came to me at that moment has changed the way I see ministry. It became for me a life-changing moment, a moment when the Lord intervened and changed my way of thinking so that I could never again pastor as I had in the past.

The Lord reminded me that what He does in the natural realm is intended to speak to us in the spiritual realm. "Yes, I put John the Baptist into the home of a priest, and I put My Son into the home of a businessman. Remember the purpose, my calling on John? He was to announce the arrival of My Son."

I began to think about John the Baptist. Even though the Bible tells us that he was unique, different, maybe even a little strange by the standards of his day, he was able to draw huge crowds when he preached. Multitudes would come to hear this strange mountain man preach his message of repentance.

My mind went to that hillside, when the crowd had gathered to hear John preach. It was becoming a common sight, this powerful man preaching and the large crowds gathering to hear his life-changing message. But he knew something, something that was very big, but he had not yet fully proclaimed it. He had hinted at his revelation throughout the opening verses of John chapter 1. He said things like, "I am not the Christ" (Jn. 1:20b), and "There stands One among you whom you do not know" (Jn. 1:26). What John knew to be the truth, and what he was getting ready to tell, was that Jesus was the Son of God.

On this—this day of destiny—he saw Jesus coming toward him, and it was different. He undoubtedly had been raised knowing Jesus, as we know his mother, Elizabeth, and Mary, Jesus' mother, were related. But on this day, he did not greet him as a friend or relative. He did not call out to his friend, "Hello, Jesus!" In fact, he did not greet Jesus at all. Instead he directed his words to the crowd. He pointed his finger at Jesus and said, "Behold! The Lamb of God who takes away the sin of the world!" (Jn. 1:29b)

At that moment John released the words for which he had been born, words that would change the course of history—for he pointed men to Jesus. John was a forerunner, an announcer. He was to proclaim that the answer was in Jesus.

The next day as John stood with two of his disciples, he again saw Jesus, and again he said, "Behold the Lamb of God!" (Jn. 1:36b) The Bible says, "The two disciples heard him speak, and they followed Jesus" (Jn. 1:37). This was John's life message. And it changed the life of Andrew, Peter's brother, that day. Andrew found his brother Peter, and on-and-on the message has gone. John fulfilled his destiny. He was not concerned about the big crowds, the popularity. He wanted to point men to Jesus.

Revival Through the Marketplace

What the Lord whispered into my spirit that day was this: "That is still the purpose for My priests. They are to announce the coming revival. And as it was with My Son, born into the home of a king, a businessman, my purpose for the kings is to bring that revival in. I will use them, the business and professional people, CEOs and employees, to bring in the harvest."

That hit me hard. For over a dozen years, Wilma and I have believed God for revival. The Bible tells us there is an endtime revival; we have no trouble believing that. The prophetic words had been consistent and regular, "Revival is coming, and you have a role to play in it." We began our congregation as a church hungering for revival, praying for revival, believing God for revival. We have desired revival so strongly, that we have said from the beginning, "If revival comes to the church down the street, we will close our doors and join them." We have said that because we have no desire to build a great church, or to develop a great ministry; we want to see and experience the work of God, and anything less is unsatisfactory.

Equipping the Kingly Saints

My desire for revival was so strong that it motivated almost our entire ministry. Coupled with the many prophetic words that had been spoken, I thought maybe it would break out in our church—maybe even while I was preaching. But as the Lord gently prodded me that December morning, I remembered how Paul had spoken in Ephesians chapter 4 regarding the equipping of the saints for the work of ministry. I was shaken as I realized how little training we were doing to release the kings into ministry. We were talking about revival, praying for revival, but not preparing for revival. I had even taught a course in our school of ministry about the equipping of the saints. But I had not been equipping anyone for ministry in the marketplace.

In my years as a pastor, my staff has developed many equipping programs for our congregations. Almost all the programs were designed to equip the saints to work in our church. We trained Sunday school teachers and youth workers, we trained ushers and worship leaders, we even trained in the field of evangelism so that members would be ready to help with the church outreach projects. We trained cell group leaders, and asked them to pastor their part of the flock. Again, it was a local church-based ministry. However, if we want to see the revival that is soon coming, we must move outside the walls of the local church.

Speaking directly to those readers who are businesspeople: Very little of our training and equipping was to send you forth into the marketplace. And for that I repent. If it were possible, I would get on my knees before you right now and ask for forgiveness on behalf of Christian leaders, who, like me, have failed to equip and release the saints for the work of ministry. I am happy to report that things are changing today. God is raising up the equippers, and God is sending forth an army of men and women into the marketplace with the power and anointing to bring revival. In the last chapter of this book, we will talk about one strategy they are using all over the world.

Who Are the Kings?

Who are these business and professional people I have been speaking about? Some will ask, "Do you have to be the CEO of a company to be a king? Does this kingly calling and anointing have to do with position, status, money, and that sort of thing?" My answer is, "No." You can be currently working for minimum wage at a temporary job and be a king. David was anointed as king long before he took his throne. God had looked on his heart and chosen him even while Saul was still on the throne. That is the case with many today. In some cases, no one else even knows what God has put in your heart. But you know. Like David, wait until the right moment, and He will release you into your kingly anointing and ministry.

So who are these "kings" that will lead us in the coming harvest? One is a taxi driver in La Plata, Argentina. He was driving me to my speaking engagements in his city and we began to talk about seeing one's business as ministry. He said he desired this, so I prayed for him, and declared him a "king." "Your taxi is your ministry, and God wants to use you through it," I told him. I saw him again four months later and he excitedly told me, "I have had the opportunity to lead someone to Christ every day since you prayed for me. It really does work. My business is my ministry."

Yes, he is one of the kings, and so are you! CEO and manager, administrator and assistant, computer programmer and custodian. Politician and plumber, football player or interior designer, God is looking on your heart. He wants to use you in reaching your city for Himself. He wants to use you to spark a revival that will change and transform your city.

Pastors, missionaries, evangelists, teachers, prophetic people, apostolic leaders—hear me well. We have an equipping task that must be completed in these last days. We must take up the mantle that has been given into our hands, and release the kings into ministry.

Chapter Three

Ordaining the Kings

Therefore, brethren, seek out from among you seven men of good reputation, full of the Holy Spirit and wisdom, whom we may appoint over this business (Acts 6:3).

They were lined up expectantly that Sunday morning, dozens of ordination candidates, ready to submit their lives to the Lord as full-time ministers. They believed that God could use them to demonstrate the gospel of the Kingdom in a way that could bring in the endtime harvest. These were business and professional leaders who had discovered that "their businesses were their ministries" and they were committing them—all of them—to God. Seldom have I seen such a serious, radically committed, spiritually pumped group of people in my life.

As I looked at them, I recalled the recommendations, a required part of the ordination process, that had come from their work associates, many of whom were non-Christians. One person wrote of their associate: "He has restored the good name of Christianity in our workplace." Another, who wrote of the mother and her two adult daughters who all work at the same company, said: "The word is out that things happen when you get on the McKain girls' prayer list." A man had written about his boss, a woman who ran a sales department for a high tech company in the Silicon Valley. He described it as "a high-pressure environment" and said she "would not allow him to tell half truths." Her commitment to integrity in the marketplace had caused him to "start thinking about spiritual things."

Seeing these candidates that morning, I realized they were not really a new breed. Rather, they were a newly released group of ministers who fit into the categories of many individuals from the Old and New Testaments who had found God's call and lived it out in the context of their daily work. Here was a group of men and women who were ready to take on California's Silicon Valley. They were no longer content to just work; they were going to minister. The weapons of their warfare were intimacy with God, intercession, integrity, moral character, passion for the lost, and compassion for the hurting. They were committed to building relationships with those who needed Jesus, and they carried one additional powerful weapon in their hands—blessing. As Ed Silvoso often says, "In the celestial game of poker, a hand of blessing beats a hand of cursing every time." And so here they were, without judgment or wrath, having completed a year of training, ready to commit their lives to serving as ministers in the marketplace. Later in this book, we will speak more of the training they received.

Blurting the Truth

The idea for the ordination had come about quite unexpectedly. What I had thought to be a couple of messages to business and professional leaders about making their business their ministry, had turned into an ongoing series of messages. In the middle of one of these, I was proclaiming, "You are in the ministry. The call of God is for all of us. God did not call just a select few. He has called you. Your business is your ministry." My next words were totally unplanned, but I believe they were from God. "Since you are called of God into the ministry of business, we should ordain you. In fact, this year we will ordain the kings."

As I realized later what I had said, I also realized I had no idea how to go about such a process. We had ordained a number of pastors and missionaries; I had a paradigm for that kind of ordination. But how do you ordain the business and professional person? And of even greater importance, is it biblical? These questions ran through my mind without an answer. Still, I believed that God had prompted those words, and as I began to study again the biblical concept of ordination, I became even more convinced. Yes, God really does have a very special plan for the business and professional Christian, and it is quite appropriate from a biblical context to ordain, to set apart those that are answering that call.

Ordination in the Bible

Ordination is something that is quite common in the church today. In fact, in the United States, it is very helpful for those in priestly ministry when it comes tax time. And yet, when the Bible uses the word *ordain*, it can refer to a thing as often as to a person. For instance, we are told in Psalm 8:2 that the Lord has "ordained strength" out of the mouths of babes to silence the enemy and the avenger. Also we are told that feasts are ordained (see 1 Kings 12:32-33), and we read that Jeremiah was ordained a prophet (see Jer. 1:5). Prophets, feasts, and strength—all ordained by God to fulfill His specially designed purpose.

In the New Testament we find that Jesus was ordained by God to be judge of the living and the dead (see Acts 10:42; 17:31), and that God has ordained His special, hidden wisdom (see 1 Cor. 2:7). In First Corinthians 7:17, Paul used the word *ordain* to speak of a directive he was giving to all the churches.

The Greek word for *ordain* is often translated "appoint," as we find in Acts 6:3. The apostles were having problems with the food program, so they set aside seven men to make sure that all were treated fairly. This story, along with the one about Saul and Barnabas in Acts 13:1-3, are two of the most commonly used to illustrate ordination today.

One night in worship, the Lord led me to Acts chapter 6, which shows a biblical way to ordain the kings.

Five Principles for Ordaining Kings

Who are these men? We must determine it from the text in Acts 6.

1. We know that they were not apostles.
2. It is obvious that they were members of the church, because the apostles said to "seek out from among you" (Acts 6:3).
3. It is likely, and I believe a very fair interpretation of the text, to say that they were businessmen in Jerusalem. The Thompson Chain Reference Bible refers to Stephen as "The Spirit-Filled Business Man."

Why do I make this point? Because I believe it is important for us to see that these are not clergy types at all. They were men from the church, men who had their training in a field that had nothing to do with a priestly type of ministry. In addition to that, the apostles sought them out to assist in a business type of activity. The apostles recognized that their own calling was in preaching and prayer. *In the same manner, they recognized a calling on these men that was in the area of business; a gifting or anointing for business was evident in their lives.*

These seven men are commonly called "deacons," but that title is not evident in the text. I have heard for years the phrase, "the seven deacons," but when I searched the Bible for evidence that these were "deacons," I could not find it. I assume someone started calling them deacons because that title corresponded with the idea that all ministry must be local church-based. If they are deacons, then we have a place to fit them in our thinking. However, the term deacon is nowhere applied to them. Acts 21:8 refers to "...the house of Philip the evangelist, who was one of the seven...."

So while they were not deacons, they did qualify for a setting aside, or appointment to a special ministry. What I began to see were the qualifications for ordination into the ministry of business and the professions. Acts chapter 6 lists five criteria for ordination. These are:

1. "Seek out from among you." It is necessary that we ordain those that we have a spiritual authority over, those within our own body.
2. "Of good reputation." Since this is for ordination in the marketplace, the reputation must extend to the workplace as well as the Christian community.
3. "Full of the Holy Spirit." Not just baby believers; and not carnal.
4. "Full of wisdom." Not having made multiple mistakes in the life of business.
5. "Full of faith." Not people who doubt God, nor who vacillate back and forth in their faith.

Application for Ordination

From those biblical criteria for ordination, I developed an application for ordination into the marketplace ministry. Each of the candidates had to submit three recommendations attesting to his or her "good reputation"—especially in the context of the marketplace. Second, they were to state their involvement in our local congregation, including their commitment to tithing. The Bible speaks clearly about the tithe, and we did not want to ordain those that were not faithful to this principle. The other three points were to be covered within the applicant's written testimony. The first section was to cover the experience of the filling of the Spirit and how this affected their ministry in the marketplace. The second would be regarding the insight God had given them concerning how they might be used to fulfill the coming marketplace revival. The last section would cover their faith in God's power to bring about this revival.

The Ordination Ceremony

On a December Sunday of that year, they stood before us, ready to be ordained. We had prepared very prayerfully for this day. On the platform of the sanctuary, we had placed a throne. Around it we poured kernels of corn, symbolic of the harvest, and placed purple bags filled with corn. These were symbolic of each candidate's individual portion of the harvest. At the end of the service, each one would go to the throne, kneel down to receive the ordination from the Lord, and have their hands filled with commissioning from the Lord.

Based on the model of King David, we would also give three anointings this morning. The first, like David's anointing by Samuel, would be a recognition of the call of God. It would be administered by a medical doctor and his wife who serve the Lord in Asia. They anointed the candidates' hands with oil. The pastors administered the second anointing, like David's anointing over the house of Judah, by anointing their heads with oil. The final anointing was at the throne, and would correspond to David's anointing over Israel. It was the actual launch into the ministry.

As these men and women knelt at the throne to receive from the Lord, we sensed something was about to break forth in the heavenly realms. This was—is—a new day, a day when ministry is to be done by the entire Body of Christ. It is a day in which ministry is moved out of the church building and into the marketplace. The nameless, faceless crowd, like the 70 sent out by Jesus in Luke chapter 10, are coming. They are being released.

And as you read this book, understand that you, too, can take part in bringing in this great harvest of souls. The call of God is for you.

Chapter Four

A Businessman Sparks a Revival

And Stephen, full of faith and power, did great wonders and signs among the people (Acts 6:8).

One day, I had just finished speaking to a group of kings when one of the young men came up to talk to me. He thanked me for the message, then told me he had cried himself to sleep almost every night since he had become a Christian a few years earlier. When I inquired as to why, he said that he very strongly desired to be in the ministry, and had asked God to release him from his job as a computer programmer. But God had not. His job in computers was greatly blessed, and there were no opportunities for him in what he considered "ministry" areas.

As he listened to the message that afternoon in Argentina, God gently spoke to him about the fact that he was in the ministry; it was the ministry of business. "Thank you so much," he said, closing our conversation, "because tonight, for the first time in years, I will go to sleep in peace knowing that God has allowed me to be in the ministry." He had traveled to Argentina looking for a touch from God, and found it in ways that he had not expected.

In 1988 my wife and I had our lives dramatically impacted and changed forever in the nation of Argentina. The nation was and still is experiencing a time of revival. In that revival atmosphere our hearts were very open to the Lord, and He filled us with a new love for Him, a desire for greater intimacy with Him. We developed a burning desire to see a nation-transforming move of God come to our city and nation as well.

Revivals Led by "Kings"

When I began studying and praying about the ministry of business and professional people, I was doing it with a revival mindset. Still, I was quite surprised to see how so many of the revivals throughout the Bible were led by "kings." When I use the word *king* here, I am using it as I have been in this book to refer to those who were not priests. Some of these, such as Nehemiah, had another profession. Nehemiah was a cup-bearer to the king. He was used of the Lord to usher in a revival that is recorded in Nehemiah chapters 8–10. Even though I had been more than a casual observer of the revivals in the Bible, it had not caught my attention that, throughout history, many of these great moves of the Lord were led by men and women who were not in the professional ministry. Consider this partial list of Old Testament revivals:

Moses in Exodus chapters 32–33
David in Second Samuel chapter 6
Jehoshaphat in Second Chronicles chapter 20
Hezekiah in Second Chronicles chapters 29–31
Josiah in Second Chronicles chapters 34-35
Nehemiah in Nehemiah chapters 8–10

In light of this initial observation, the idea of "ordaining" some of the kings in our local church was born out of a desire to honor the calling in the kings and to set them apart to fulfill their calling. As I started to study about ordination, I was surprised again by what I discovered. What I found made me even more convinced that the Lord was revealing something very special about His plan for business and professional people.

My study on ordination took me to the Book of Acts, especially to chapter 6. It was in the context of that chapter that we developed a process for ordaining the business and professional people in our congregation.

A New Testament Businessman Sparks Revival

Now, let us return to the story of Stephen in Acts as we consider the "kings" role in revival. The Church was growing rapidly in Jerusalem during those days. Before violent persecution broke out against the Christians, there were internal problems. Because Jews who accepted Jesus as Messiah were sometimes cut off from their families, the believers had to learn how to work together and, out of necessity, depended on each other for support. When we read in Acts 2:44 that they "had all things in common," this was not only a reality, but a reality born of deep need. The sharing of homes, food, and resources became a mark of the early Church partly because there was no other way for them to survive. As the Church continued to grow, it became necessary to organize the sharing. However, some were being overlooked, which created a situation that had all the hallmarks of racial discrimination. There were complaints. The problem needed to be solved.

The apostles came up with a plan which was developed out of their own understanding that they should not leave their major calling. They were to continue to preach and pray, rather than spending precious time resolving the issue. So they determined to find a group of seven men who would be chosen for their integrity, faith, wisdom, and Spirit-filled life. These men would take on the task of administrating the food program. I think it is safe to say that these men would be entrusted not only with the program, but also with the administration of the money to operate it. It is interesting to me that the wording in the Bible is that they chose these seven to "appoint over this business." The words *appoint* or *ordain* and *business* are connected in this text.

When they had found suitable men, they laid hands on them and appointed, or ordained them for the task. There is no reference to how the seven men resolved the problem, but there is also no further reference to the problem. This is what happens when businesspeople get involved; they are able to solve what appear to be insurmountable problems very simply. It is a part of their gifting.

Soon after the apostles laid their hands on them, a new wave of revival broke out. I want to make sure that you see what happened here. One day the apostles called for a special meeting of the Church. Stephen, along with many others, responded and attended this meeting. The apostles informed the congregation of a problem—they needed some help with the food distribution program. Stephen was selected as one of those to assist in the project. They called him forward along with six others, and the apostles laid hands on them. As we follow the text, the next thing that happened was more growth in the Church; the number of disciples multiplied and even a number of priests were obedient. Without reference to the passing of time, the text next indicates that Stephen was doing signs and wonders. I do not know how much later it was, but it was not long. The same day? Very likely.

Stephen had been a good church member, faithful and of good reputation. Suddenly, he was pushed to the front lines. Not only did the Church grow, but also Stephen experienced the manifestation of miracles through his ministry. Out on the streets, out in the marketplace, the power of God broke through.

Stephen was not appointed to do wonders and signs. He was appointed as an administrator of the food program. The Bible never informs us of what even happened with the food ministry. What went on? The reality is that as soon as the early Church called forth the Spirit-filled business leader, things started to happen. I can't help but wonder what will happen in our churches today when we recognize the gifts and callings on these kings that God is raising up. When you release a businessman, a king, into his anointing, you can never tell what might happen.

In Argentina, a revival broke out when a businessman named Carlos Annacondia started preaching. Even though he has been preaching for more than a dozen years, Annacondia still derives his income from his business. This does not mean that you must become a preacher. I am just pointing out what may happen when a businessperson is released to fulfill the call of God.

Modern Examples

It was Wesley who said, "The world is my parish." He was being criticized for taking the gospel outside the church, but he recognized the need to impact all sectors of society. Today, men like Chuck Colson are illustrating the effectiveness of kingly ministry in prisons, and business leaders like John Beckett are setting the pace in the marketplace. Beckett's book, *Loving Monday*, is helping business leaders to succeed in business without selling their souls. He himself is very successful in business, and he has continued to operate in that setting without compromising his Christian principles. But he is also successful in ministry, for the marketplace provides great opportunities to impact communities and even nations for Christ. On a recent visit to Beckett's companies in Ohio, I observed that his faith and his work are integrated, and those who work for him know it.

In New York City in 1857, a revival broke out when a businessman named Jeremiah Lanphier started a noontime prayer meeting. His church had appointed him as a "city missionary," and not knowing what to do, he prayed a simple prayer: "Lord, what wilt Thou have me to do?" The answer to that prayer led him to start a prayer meeting that would ultimately see one million souls brought to Jesus. Led by a businessman, it was a prayer revival that impacted cities across America, Canada, England, Scotland, and Wales. It sounds like Stephen all over again.

Where did this man Stephen learn how to preach? And why did he preach? As soon as I mention that Stephen preached, there is an assumption by some that he left the business world and entered the ministry to become a preacher. But that is not the case with Stephen, and it need not be the case today. Acts 6:8 tells us that Stephen "did great wonders and signs." Where did he do these wonders and signs? The answer is "among the people." This was a miraculous ministry that broke out on the streets—perhaps it might have occurred in the context of Stephen's work. The Bible does not tell us that, and I do not want to try to make it say something it does not, but I believe the day is coming when God will move with power in businesses, schools, shopping malls, and neighborhoods.

So why did Stephen preach? He probably didn't set out to preach. He was simply operating in the new anointing that came on him through the laying on of hands. Suddenly he was operating in the miraculous—wonders and signs. In the daily activities of his life, he began to see the power of God in new and awesome ways.

Godly Businesspeople Face Opposition

If God starts using you to perform the miraculous, there will be some opposition. When the opposition came for Stephen, he responded with such wisdom that it could not be resisted (see Acts 6:10). His preaching was simply a by-product of the power of God that came into his life.

As a result of performing the miraculous, the forces of religious tradition were immediately threatened and began to debate and dispute over what he had done. Yet they were not able to resist the intelligence, wisdom, and inspiration imparted to Stephen, a man of good and attested character.

When the religious spirit of "the law" was powerless to resist the flow of the Holy Spirit through Stephen, the fallback position was to slander and otherwise incite others against this power. A turf battle ensued that threatened the institutional church of the day, and it was in response to the resultant outcry that Stephen preached. His message was not one that was studied or outlined in advance. There was no time for that. Instead, out of the fullness of his heart, he proclaimed the truth. His message was basically, "It is not surprising that God would work in my life in this way; He has always had a people." Stephen goes on to preach what will be the longest message recorded in the Book of Acts, and by the time we reach the end of chapter 7, he has become the first martyr for the Christian faith.

As we move into chapter 8, Stephen is buried. Nevertheless, the gospel moves out of Jerusalem and into Samaria. As the Church is scattered, we notice that the apostles stay in Jerusalem. So it was the kings whom God raised up to lead the next wave of missionary movement. One of the leaders is another of these Spirit-filled businessmen, Philip. Philip began in Samaria where he likewise experienced the manifestation of the miraculous in his ministry. He is led by an angel to minister to another leader from the "kingly" ranks, a man holding great authority under the queen of Ethiopia, and in charge of her treasury. Suddenly, the potential for widespread revival becomes a reality through only one day in the ministry of one of God's most anointed businessman preachers ever.

How did it all start? Well, according to the Scripture, Stephen was simply one of the multitude. Paul Cain has stated on numerous occasions that he believes that the coming revival will be led by a team of "nameless, faceless leaders." That is exactly what Stephen had been; he was an unknown. Cain has served the Lord in a powerful prophetic anointing for years. He has been at our church and I've experienced firsthand the tremendous insight the Lord gives to him. He is one of God's very humble and very powerful servants, and has been around long enough to see many of the great evangelists of the 1950's right down to today.

Even though we may say Stephen was an unknown, it is obvious that the Lord knew him and that he knew the Lord. It is also obvious that when given the opportunity to speak about one of their own, the Church knew him. I can imagine one of the new Christians in the Jerusalem church saying something like this to the apostles: "You need help? Stephen is your man! He is full of the Holy Ghost, honest in every business practice; he is a man you can trust."

How many "Stephens" are there in our churches today—just members of the church, just one of the crowd, just a businessperson—that is, until we look closer? On closer examination, we find a group of wise and respected, Spirit-filled individuals just waiting for a release—a release that brings the understanding that you can minister under the anointing of the Holy Spirit in the marketplace. You need to begin to see your workplace as a place to honor and serve the Lord. Start by doing all of your tasks as "unto the Lord." "And *whatever* you do in word or deed, *do* all in the name of the Lord Jesus, giving thanks to God the Father through Him" (Col. 3:17). "Whatever you do, do all to the glory of God" (1 Cor. 10:31b). There is an anointing for creativity, productivity, and prosperity. There is also a time and an anointing to proclaim the Word with boldness. Remain sensitive to the leading of the Holy Spirit.

Businesspeople as God's Heroes

Is Stephen an exception? Or is he an example of how God has worked in times past and therefore desires to work today? We can gain some very powerful insight and possibly even the answer to those questions by carefully reading the sermon that Stephen preached as recorded in Acts chapter 7. This message is really a rehearsal of the history of the nation of Israel, and their resistance and rebellion against God. Stephen makes it clear that there was never a time when the entire nation worshiped God, but there was always a small remnant of true believers—even as there is in our day. To make his point, he tells the story of three of God's heroes:

1. Abraham   vs. 1-8
2. Joseph   vs. 9-16
3. Moses   vs. 17-45

Included in the message there is also the brief mentioning of Isaac, Jacob, Aaron, David, and Solomon.

Abraham

Stephen began his message by talking about Abraham. This would make perfect sense to a Jew, for to him history began with Abraham.

Abraham was a man who answered God's summons. He did not know where he was going, but nevertheless believed that under God's direction, the best was yet to come. He is a great example of faith and hope, as well. Even when he had no children, and humanly speaking it seemed impossible that he would ever have any, he believed that one day his descendants would inherit the land that God gave to them.

Joseph

The key to Joseph's life can be summed up in his own words in Genesis 50:20: "But as for you, you meant evil against me; but God meant it for good...." His brothers were afraid that after the death of Jacob, Joseph would take vengeance on them for what they had done to him. Joseph, however, was a man who listened to God—and forgave. Stephen sums up his life with these words: "But God was with him and delivered him out of all his troubles, and gave him favor and wisdom..." (Acts 7:9b-10).

Moses

Like Abraham and Joseph, Moses was a man who answered God's command to go out. He gave up a kingdom to answer God's summons to lead His people. All three of these men were ready to leave comfort and ease to follow the Lord wherever He might lead.

As Stephen continued with his message, he became very direct and offensive to the high priests who had confronted him and challenged him with the question: "Are these things so?" in Acts 7:1. This question was necessary because of the accusations thrown at Stephen after his powerful ministry in Jerusalem following his ordination. Stephen became the first martyr for the Christian faith, and the blood that he shed became fertilizer for the revival that would move out of Jerusalem and ultimately go into the entire world.

I know that every detail of the Word of God is important, and that I have not given an adequate exposition of Acts 7. But there is a detail that I think is easy to miss if we get caught up with all the other details.

This has to do, not with the content of the message of Stephen, not with the result of the message, but with the style of the message. Stephen's style is to use people to relate the history of God's movement throughout the Old Testament. I have mentioned a few things about these three men, Abraham, Joseph, and Moses. But who are they in terms of profession?

Abraham was a businessman, cattle rancher, landowner, and an investor in silver and gold (see Gen. 13).

Joseph was successful and prosperous (see Gen. 39:2), a manager (see Gen. 39:4), second in command and ruler over all of Egypt at age 30 (see Gen. 41:40), and a manager of an immense warehousing system (see Gen. 41:48).

Moses also was a businessman, who was raised as royalty (see Ex. 2:10), managed his father-in-law's flocks (see Ex. 3:1), was called by God to lead the children of Israel out of Egypt (see Ex. 3:15 and following), and of course became a leader, strategist, and manager through his experiences with the Israelites.

Stephen uses three businessmen as the symbols for God's activity in the entire Old Testament.

Miracles for Today

In Acts chapters 6 through 8 we have one businessman who sparks a revival in his hometown, and is the instrument through which God does miraculous signs and wonders. He is the first other than the apostles to have such a ministry. Today there are many who are saying that the ministry of signs and wonders disappeared with the apostles. Stephen and Philip stand in opposition to that, and bring a tremendous hope for an equally powerful ministry today.

In addition, this same man who experienced the power of God on his life, in only one day became the spark for a national revival, as well as the one in his own city. He did this partially by outlining the ministries of three other businessmen who were used so greatly by God that Stephen sees their story as the one that is best descriptive of history.

In Acts chapter 8, we see the ministry of Philip, another businessman anointed for revival. He was one whom God raised up during the time the apostles still stayed in Jerusalem. But God had work to do, and used Philip to reach multitudes. He had a powerful deliverance ministry and the people were amazed at the miracles he did.

God used him to reach both a high-profile sorcerer and a highly-placed government official. I keep seeing this picture of God doing the same in our day.

God is at work, and He is working through more than pastors and professional evangelists. He is at work in the business and professional people, the kings that He has raised up for this day. He is at work in many places outside of the church buildings and regularly scheduled church meetings; God is at work in the marketplace.

Currently in our world there are a number of revivals that are drawing worldwide attention. Those who want to visit the revival in Toronto, go to a church. The same is true for the powerful move of God in Pensacola, Florida. It is housed in a church. The revival in Argentina is also church-based, with the exception of the huge tent crusades that are led by the evangelist Carlos Annacondia. Guatemala? Same story! Awesome move of God, thousands coming to faith in Christ every week. Do you want to see it? You can, and you will visit a church to do so. How about Korea? You already know the answer. Around the world God is moving in revival, church-based revival.

This is not the revival I envision. No, the one I see will take place in a business. Possibly a lunchtime prayer meeting will surprise even its leaders, and begin to impact the entire business. I can imagine a conversation around the coffee machine where one of God's kings notices the hopeless look on the face of a friend. As he asks the reason for the discouragement, the report from the doctor is recounted, "It's cancer, and there is not much hope." In my vision I see the king praying—and the miraculous answer. As word of this spreads through the company, a weekly, or even daily, revival starts around the coffee machine. The CEO of the company is not bothered by the meetings, and even supports them, for he too has received a touch from God.

Or maybe the revival breaks out in a department store as the musician on the grand piano plays an old hymn, and suddenly people are falling on their knees in repentance. It could happen at a nightclub when suddenly the Spirit of God descends on the place and everyone receives a spiritual touch. It could be in the locker room of a major league team, or in a local high school. What I know is this, God says it will happen. "...in the last days, says God, that I will pour out of My Spirit on all flesh" (Acts 2:17a).

"All flesh."

Those who will receive this outpouring are not all in our churches, and it is unlikely they are all going to come. But they will be somewhere: at work, at school, at the mall, in the park, on the street corner. Wherever they are, that is where God is, pouring out His Spirit!

And who will tell them of the love of God? Who will demonstrate the power of the Resurrection? You will. God can and will use you. The exciting thing is, He will use you right where you are. Can you imagine your work, your job, your business becoming a tool for revival? Well, get used to the idea, because it is in the heart of God!

Chapter Five

Your Business in City-Reaching

Do business till I come (Luke 19:13b).

Recently, while I was in Guatemala studying Spanish, I was accompanying the director of our school on a bus trip to a nearby city. As we passed through the city of Almolonga, I noticed a line of women carrying huge baskets of vegetables on their heads. The scene is not uncommon in Guatemala, except that this line of women was blocks long, and the vegetables were unusually large. I recognized the name of the city as one where Harold Caballeros, my friend from Guatemala City, had recently preached. As I was not sure of the name of the church at which Harold might have preached, I asked if there was a large church in town. The director told me that there were several large churches in town. In fact, he thought maybe ten or more had over 1,000 members. Imagine that! A city with a population of only 18,000 was home to ten churches of over 1,000.

When I was able to talk to Pastor Harold about Almolonga, he told me an amazing story. Once one of the poorest cities in the nation, Almolonga is now one of the most prosperous. Its extreme poverty was exacerbated by a very high rate of alcoholism. One day the wife of one of the local alcoholics convinced the pastor to pray for her husband as he slept off his most recent drinking binge. God chose to deliver the man from alcohol while he was asleep, and he awoke a new man. Soon this was happening to others, and the transformation was under way.

Over a period of a few years, the bars closed and churches grew. And not only that, God did an amazing thing in the fields surrounding this agricultural city. He began to water the crops from underground. The vegetables grew increasingly larger, denser, and more delicious. The city known for its poverty became the richest city around. Where poverty had ruled for years, prosperity was the norm. The jail has closed, as it is no longer needed, and over 90 percent of the population are now Christians. Almolonga is a city transformed by a mighty move of God's Spirit.

Seeing the Needs Around You

We need to start dreaming bigger dreams, and making bigger plans. Ed Silvoso has affected my thinking on this matter. His book, *That None Should Perish*,[1] is about reaching cities through prayer evangelism. During my early years as a pastor, my major goal was for our church to grow. There is certainly nothing wrong with that, but if it stops there, we will miss God's greater desire. God wants us to reach our city, not fill our church building.

Even though we eventually filled our building on Sunday morning, and grew to two, three, and finally four services each Sunday, we were not reaching our city; and anything short of city transformation is unsatisfactory. Many of my pastor friends have discovered that as well and now also focus on reaching their cities.

You can imagine my joy when I found a Bible passage with this exact focus, and which gives the authority for reaching the city to business leaders. The city was Jericho, but it could just as easily be your city. The city-reacher in this case was Jesus. Let us visit the city of Jericho and watch Jesus in action. He has a powerful word for business leaders.

Chapter divisions in the Bible are sometimes not helpful, and I think this is the case in Luke chapter 19. Let us begin reading at

Luke 18:35 so we don't miss some valuable insights into Jesus' method for reaching the city.

Jesus came to Jericho accompanied by a crowd. As He was entering the city, a blind man sat by the roadside, begging. Luke does not tell us his name, but from Mark's account we know his name was Bartimaeus. As he heard the multitude coming his way, he asked what was going on. Being informed that Jesus was coming his way, he began to cry out to the Lord. However, those who followed Jesus on that day (could they be likened to the Church?) warned him to be quiet.

I have been a pastor for long enough to know that schedules and programs are "really important." But I have missed God many times because I would not be deterred from time constraints or established programs. It would appear that the crowd around Jesus was acting a lot like I have.

To them it was more important to stay on schedule than to accommodate a poor, begging, blind man. They must have thought they were assisting Jesus in keeping to His agenda, and were committed to getting Him to Jericho on time. But usually it is not His agenda that we are interested in; it is our own agenda.

Jesus was not in a hurry, not at all. The truth is that this man was a part of His agenda, His target audience in the city of Jericho. Jesus' first priority upon entering the city was the poor. A beggar received His full attention, and no other issue could take precedence. Jesus stopped everything to see what He could do for the blind beggar.

God Meets Our Greatest Needs

It strikes me as interesting that the man was begging, and yet when asked by Jesus what he wanted, he made no reference to money or food. He knew enough about Jesus to request the higher need: "Lord that I may receive my sight" (Lk. 18:41b). If Jesus were to look you in the face, and ask you, "What do you want Me to do for you?" what would you say? You need to think about it, because it is in the Father's heart to give you your desires. Have you learned to ask Jesus for the higher thing, or are you still simply asking

Him for money and food. Listen to your prayers and see what it is that you are asking the Lord for.

It is a little disconcerting to realize that more fasting is done for money and resources than for souls. Bartimaeus knew that he had a higher need and went for that, his sight. In the process, he received not only his sight but his other needs as well, as we will see in a few moments.

Once Jesus had healed the man, the crowd accepted him, and were willing to welcome him into their midst. Earlier, they were not so excited about bringing in a man with an obvious need. "Oh Lord, help us see the hurting through Your eyes, to focus on the poor as a first priority in our target audience."

As we walk with Jesus along the road to Jericho, we see His next priority. Coming into the city, He was confronted by a rich man named Zacchaeus (see Lk. 19:1-10). He had the same problem that blind Bartimaeus had—he could not see. In his case, it was not blindness that caused his lack of sight, but instead it was the crowd. They were so tightly packed around the Savior that those on the outside could not see Him.

Many times we believers are so happy inside the four walls of the church, that even those in our own neighborhoods have trouble seeing Jesus in us. How can they? We are never out in the streets. Ministry has become more a process of hiding behind the walls of our buildings than in making Jesus visible in our neighborhoods. Like those surrounding Jesus, we can be more of a detriment than a help in assisting Jesus in the fulfillment of His plan for the city.

Now notice this: Jesus did not target only the poor; He was equally interested in the rich. "Lord, help us to see that the rich are also hurting, and need to see Jesus."

Both groups are equally important to Him, and I believe that it is the Lord's desire for the poor and rich to worship together, to stand next to each other as they lift their praise to the Lord, learning to serve Him together. As I have studied the roles of the kings in the Old Testament, I've found one of the major callings was to lift injustice and to remove oppression. The kings are to be leading out in ministering to the poor.

As Zacchaeus came down from his perch in the tree—the only place he could find to get a glimpse of Jesus—the disciples encountered another problem. Jesus invited Himself to dinner with this sinner. I guarantee you that if you stick around most congregations long enough, you too will forget what it is to associate with sinners.

Making Sinner Friends

Most of my friends are pastors, missionaries, and church leaders. I need some sinner friends! (I said that in one church in Monterrey, Mexico, and was surprised when a girl raised her hand. I asked her what she wanted and she said, "I will be your sinner friend." After the service I talked to her and found that she was a non-Christian, and a first-time visitor to the church. In the same way I needed a sinner friend, she needed a Christian friend.) That is why I am so thrilled that God is raising up a new group of leaders for this coming move of God. Those of you who serve the Lord in the marketplace are already accustomed to daily contact with unbelievers. It makes sense, does it not, that the Lord would choose to use those in the closest contact with the harvest to bring that harvest in?

Jesus was not afraid to make friends of sinners, whether they were poor or rich. They were the ones that He first sought out in Jericho. I have to believe He does the same today, in my city and yours. It is time for us to begin to focus on the same audience. The ones who do not yet know the Lord need to experience His love. And Jesus was able to do this without any condemnation. You will not see Him explaining to either Bartimaeus or Zacchaeus that they are lost and going to hell. Instead, we see Jesus ministering love and compassion. To the blind man, He asked, "What do you want Me to do for you?" (Mk. 10:51) To Zacchaeus He simply said, "Today salvation has come to this house, because he also is a Son of Abraham" (Lk. 19:9).

Reaching Out to Your Own—Miracles Can Happen!

Zacchaeus made some very significant decisions about his lifestyle very early in his relationship with Jesus. We do not know what Jesus said to him, if anything, but simply being in the presence of Jesus caused this man to do some very radical things.

While the disciples were still fuming over the fact that Jesus was associating with a sinner, the sinner in question was doing some very spiritual things. He immediately decided to give half his goods to the poor. The Bible does not tell us that Jesus told him to do that. He might have, but it is also possible that He mentioned nothing at all. I have certainly experienced times when simply being in the presence of Jesus caused me to do some significant things. Whatever the process, whatever means the Lord used to impact Zacchaeus, the result was that he was giving to the poor.

Imagine the reaction of the crowd which included, of course, those that had followed Him into the city of Jericho, and the recently healed blind man who had been sitting by the roadside. When Zacchaeus started looking for the poor to give money to, he would not have had to look far. It is not farfetched at all to presume that Bartimaeus would have been one who received that day.

Think of the moment when Jesus asked the poor man what He could do for him. If the man had simply asked for money, he conceivably could still be sitting by the road, blind and lost, but with a few dollars in his pocket. However, he was healed, walking with Jesus, and receiving his financial needs as well. Remember, Jesus is well able to take care of all your needs, but He may not do it by the process that you have prescribed, or even by a way that seems most likely to you. If He can minister healing to the blind beggar and then minister another kind of healing to a man who will start giving him money, don't you think He can take care of your needs as well?

Zacchaeus was not content with giving away just 50 percent of his money. In addition to that, he also gave back four times whatever he had taken by false accusation. Here was a rich man that had been touched to the very core of his being. For Zacchaeus, becoming a follower of Jesus meant giving away more than half of his money, and he trusted God to meet his needs as he gave.

I remember one time I was on my face before the Lord in one of our services. As I was there on the floor, I heard the Lord speak to me about giving away a car, actually it was my wife's car. I started to argue with the Lord, an argument that I was sure to lose. I said something like, "But Lord, we just finished paying for that car!" His response as I recall was, "Good, then you won't have to give away a car that you still owe money on."

That evening I told Wilma about this; it was, after all, her car. After making sure that I had in fact heard from the Lord, she agreed that we should give away the car. So, a few days later, we gave the car to the intended recipient, and then waited for the Lord to honor the seed we had sown with another car. Since I knew the principles of sowing and reaping, I was quite certain that the Lord would honor this seed very soon.

We waited for a week, and then a month. We continued waiting for a year, and eventually for two years. One day I went home and told Wilma that I had it figured out. We would just go out and buy a car and trust God to provide for the payments. She would have nothing of that, instead insisting that we wait upon the Lord and believe Him to provide. After a few more months, I had another plan. We would not buy a car; instead we would lease a car. Again, she would have no part of this plan either. Wilma was convinced that if I jumped into this situation to resolve it on my own, we would stand the chance of missing the blessing of the Lord. So we waited. Finally, over two years later, the Lord provided a brand new vehicle, without a dollar out of my pocket.

During that time of waiting, Wilma would often remind me, "You heard from the Lord, so trust Him." I send that same word to you. Let the Lord speak to you in the area of your money. The Jesus that I know is concerned about your bank account. He is fully able to fulfill His promises, and He will not ask you to do something that He will not bless.

As far as we know, Zacchaeus did not pray the sinner's prayer. There is no instruction noted in the Bible for the process by which his salvation came to pass. In fact, the only thing we know for sure is that Jesus impacted his heart and his response was to give financially. But the next verse of Scripture tells us that salvation came to his house that day.

Using Your Money for God

It is in that context that we come to a very interesting parable, a parable for the businessperson (see Lk. 19:11-27). Here Jesus' audience included those who followed Him into Jericho, plus those whom He picked up on the way. One of them was a poor blind beggar. One of them was one of the richest men in town, Zacchaeus. Both of them had their lives radically changed by the power of the Lord. Both of them, and I'm sure by this time, everyone else, were ready to hear whatever He had to say. Jesus began talking about money.

Most business leaders understand the concept of making money. Far above any other reason, that is why businesses are started. Hopefully, you have discovered that there are higher purposes for your life, and that you are no longer living with only the desire for money driving you.

It is interesting to note that Jesus had a parable set aside for the businessperson, and that parable was about making money. From this parable, I believe we can learn that Jesus wants us to make money. However, because of the very context of the parable, we know He is concerned about far more than our money. He is looking for people like Bartimaeus and Zacchaeus.

In this parable, we have the story of a certain man who went into a far country. He called ten of his servants together and gave a mina to each one of them. A mina is a sum of money that is equal to about three months' wages. Upon giving the money to his servants, he said to them, "Do *business* till I come" (Lk. 19:13)— instructions for a business and professional person. Any time you receive an amount of money with the command, "Do business till I come," you will obviously realize the serious nature of the situation.

It is time to become creative and strategic. You must invest well, work hard, plan right, and do whatever it takes to "do business" with that money.

Taking Authority Over Cities

In this parable, like so many others, some of the workers did well and some did not. But what captures my attention is what the reward was for the man who took the one mina and earned ten minas. We see in verse 17: "Because you were faithful in very little, have authority over ten cities."

Authority over cities! That is what you can gain from faithful business practices—authority in your city, and in nine cities surrounding you. Do you see the tremendous impact of this truth? When God gives you the grace to increase, to make money, He has a purpose for this. His purpose is not only to allow you to gain more, and live easier. His purpose goes beyond even the ability to give more.

He wants to give you authority!

There is tremendous authority in business today. The decision-makers and power brokers in our nation are business leaders who are looked upon as successful. There was a day when the "clergy" were looked to for advice and direction, and in some nations the military or government may carry the authority. But in America today, it is success in the business realm, economic success, that causes people to want to listen to you.

Jesus has put something in your hand: an amount of money perhaps, or an idea, or a strategy for marketing success. As He blesses this, and the one turns into ten, remember that the authority you gain is for the Kingdom. He wants you to impact cities. I originally challenged you to see your marketplace position as your ministry; but Jesus moves it several notches higher. His goal for you is *authority in the city*. Jesus is concerned about your city, your state, and your nation. And He wants to use you to impact your city for the gospel.

The time has come for the kings of the Lord to take their God-given role and change our world. We have waited too long for change to come about through political process. The Republicans take all the credit they can and cast blame on the Democrats. Simultaneously, the Democrats do the same with their particular political agenda. But caring for the poor is not a political issue; it is a Christian issue. God is putting the mandate on the shoulders of the kings to lift the oppression, care for the poor, and bring about justice and mercy in our land. This authority, this God-given authority, must be carefully and prayerfully administrated. God is raising you up for such a time as this.

This parable is not about planting churches. There are no missionary plans, nor can a single priest be found. But God is at work, using business principles and business leaders to impact entire cities for the gospel. Think about it. With just a few ten-mina leaders and another handful of five-mina leaders, we can take dozens, hundreds, even thousands of cities for Christ.

Now let's make a quick review. Jesus came to the city with an eye on the poor and rich. He brought both into the Kingdom, despite the objections of His followers. In the context of that particular crowd, the poor, the rich, the recently healed and blessed, the recently convicted, Jesus told His business parable. Business and professional leaders, don't miss the point. Yes, He wants to bless your business; He wants to help you make money; and He wants to give you authority. But it is also clear from Scripture that He wants to use you to change the status of the poor. When the poor of the inner cities and the CEOs of commerce in those same cities get together, God will release His strategic plan for impacting the cities.

Authority—Not Ability

The plan of God is connected to the authority that He will give to you. Let's think about that for a few moments because it is another key to your success in the kingly anointing. Remember, that anointing comes from the Holy One and abides in you. God takes this anointing and connects it to authority. That is an important point, because authority is something that God gives you based on His sovereignty. When we are called to accomplish something for the Lord, we may complain about our lack of ability; but

God is not looking at your ability. He is focusing on the authority that He has given you.

Remember when David was first anointed as king? He was the least likely of all his brothers to be chosen. But then the Word of the Lord came, "Man looks at the outward appearance, but the Lord looks at the heart" (1 Sam. 16:7b). We could paraphrase it this way: "Man looks at ability, but the Lord looks on the heart, knowing the authority that He will place there." You cannot argue with God. Don't try to tell Him that you can or cannot do something based on your ability. I have seen many leaders with great ability fail, because they lacked in anointing; and I have seen people of seeming little ability prosper greatly because of the anointing.

Authority!

Jesus said to His disciples, "Behold, I give you the authority...over all the power of the enemy" (Lk. 10:19a). I would much rather have authority than ability, because the anointing of God connects to that authority and "nothing shall be impossible for you who believe" (see Mk. 9:23). Those who walk in the authority of God will lead this coming marketplace revival. There will always be those who make more money than you do, and there will always be those who have more ability. But when you walk in the authority of God, nothing can stop you.

Not long ago, I received the telephone call that told me that my dad, at 88 years of age, had gone home to be with the Lord. Dad was a strong business leader, a king, and now he was gone. After the memorial service, when things had quieted down, my wife and I went back to the house in which I had been raised. I had to pick up the last of my "goods" from when I was a young boy. Among my belongings I found an old, yellowed piece of paper that was a speech evaluation from my freshman year in college. I tell you, it is amazing to think that someone could preach as long as I have with the kind of report I received in my college speech class. It proved the point that in the natural I was not called to be a public speaker.

The evaluator scored me in four ranks: superior, well done, fair, and needs improvement. I received no superior marks, four marks as well done, four marks under fair, and eight marks in the needs improvement column. Down at the bottom he had written some notes. Under "general effectiveness," he wrote, "beginning very ineffective." Then he wrote this sentence to amplify that: "Compare your development with the others, for instance, and you'll realize how much work you need to do." Whoa! I tell you...I read that and was immediately impacted. Tears came to my eyes as I realized...he was talking about me! Then he penned a recommendation: "You need to work on fluency of delivery. You need to work on variety of illustrations and development. And, you need to work on variety of sentence structure and expression." My professor had not learned the art of blessing and encouragement.

Now my point is, God didn't call me to be a preacher because of my natural ability. I was, according to my professor, "very ineffective." But when God says, "This is what I want you to do," He begins to put His anointing on you. When He calls you, He gives you His authority, and to that authority, he adds His anointing. He begins to take your inability and replaces it with His ability. He takes what you cannot do, and substitutes what He can do. The result is that you can become very, very effective. Remember, when God speaks to you and says, "This is what I want you to do," it does not necessarily mean that's what you're already good at. It means this is what He is going to enable you to do through His power.

We need to start responding to God based on His call and on His authority, not based on our ability or our understanding. Oftentimes we have no idea of what God is about to do; however, when we simply walk in obedience, He will bring about the fulfillment of His plan.

Do you see what the Lord has in mind for your business? He wants to bless it so that you gain authority. Then He wants to take the authority and add His anointing to it, so that entire cities are transformed. Although many congregations and mission agencies are involved in city-reaching plans, such as Harvest Evangelism, Mission America, and others, and there is broad cooperation in reaching these major population areas, we still need the involvement of business and professional leaders. Come on, kings! We need you to help usher in the coming city-transforming move of God!

Endnote

1. Ed Silvoso, *That None Should Perish* (Ventura, CA: Regal Books, 1994).

Chapter Six

The Role of Kings

You shall surely set a king over you whom the Lord your God chooses; one from among your brethren you shall set as king over you (Deuteronomy 17:15a).

I was recently involved in a summit that included both "kings" and "priests" who were interested in seeing their cities impacted for Christ. We brought these groups together in an effort to determine how we could better serve one another, and begin to work together to see the Kingdom of God grow on the earth.

The Lord clearly confirmed to me what I already knew about the Christian business community—this new breed of ministers is ready to go. The reality is that the marketplace is in the center of society, and any effort to reach cities must include marketplace ministry. The individuals who gathered recognized that role, and are beginning to step into it in cities across America and the world.

Both the pastors and city-reaching leaders also recognized the role the businessperson has to play in the coming move of God. God is actively working to bring both groups into unity of purpose and function.

Getting It on Paper

One of the goals I had set for the conference was to publish a paper clearly stating the role of the kings in the city-reaching effort. I had envisioned this paper being clear enough for a businessperson to hand it to his pastor and say, "I am here to serve you, and this is what I can offer."

We opened the day with some foundational, biblical teaching on the role of the business and professional leaders in the present-day marketplace. Afterward, we entered into a session of "war room strategies" to clearly state our role as kings in the marketplace and in city-reaching efforts.

I had asked Nancy Duarte, who along with her husband, Mark, owns one of Silicon Valley's key marketing firms, to facilitate this session for us. While she is used to doing this with CEOs in boardrooms, she came to this session with a different agenda in mind. She led us in a time of communion and read Isaiah 58 as the basis for where we were going. This tied in directly with the teaching we had received earlier in the day. Surely we were ready to "hear from God, and write an awesome document."

Breaking the Logjam

We started off well, but soon were divided. Everyone had good ideas, and these were coming fast, but there was no flow. The sheets on the wall were filling up, but the strategy was not becoming clear. In fact, the opposite was happening. Some were energized with excitement; others were confused. Some were feeling good; others were frustrated. Clearly, it was time to take a break, and pray.

Even during the break, we were inundated with ideas, frankly, all of them good. But the one idea we needed, the one that in our own wisdom we could not find, was the "God idea." So we began to worship and pray. The Lord seemed very pleased with this, as His presence became obvious to all of us. Mark Duarte was playing the guitar, more in a prophetic act of worship than in leading worship. As he played and we prayed, the Lord began to point in another direction.

I looked into the audience and saw David, a young man I had met earlier in the day. He had told me that he had no idea why he was there, that he was not a businessman or pastor, and had no leadership role in the Body of Christ. The Lord prompted me to call David to the front to share his testimony. What he had to say altered the meeting, drew it back to the Lord, and spoke powerfully to everyone there.

David told us that he was only two years old in the Lord, and that he had AIDS as a result of his homosexual lifestyle. He currently managed a home for victims of AIDS, and even though there were only four patients living there, three had died over the last two years. He then looked at this audience of business leaders from across the United States and challenged us with words like these: "In the home that I run, there are all kinds of governmental regulations. But you could start a home and offer the hope of the Lord Jesus from the very first day. All of the words you have put on the papers are fine, but why not just do it." He also informed us that many churches come wanting to help, but only under their own set of rules.

Something happened right then, and the Sprit of the Lord took control of the meeting from that moment on. We blessed David and prayed for his full deliverance and healing. We repented before him for the judgment that we had put on homosexuals and victims of AIDS. We cried at his feet and laid on hands in prayer. We sang blessing over David, and then we found ourselves performing a prophetic act.

Ed Silvoso had taught us earlier in the day about the power of prophetic acts. He had explained that even though we sometimes do an act that seems rather simple and meaningless in the natural, it is powerful in the spiritual realm. This is based on the teaching in John 8:44 where it tells us that the devil is a liar, and that he "does not stand in the truth, because there is no truth in him." Because of this principle, when the truth is revealed, satan's hold on individuals—or situations—is weakened. The Spirit, at the same time, can move more freely. When we do a prophetic act, we are drawing a circle of truth around the lie of the devil.

Consider the prophetic act we did that afternoon. For years the devil has told everyone that Christians would never love homosexuals. He said we would judge them, condemn them, and stay clear of them. The same, or even more so, would be true with AIDS victims. So, when we repented for our lack of love, our judgment, our haughty spirit and more, we were painting a new picture of truth. As the group began to realize what was happening, members spontaneously joined hands in a circle around David. There he stood, the object of our love and acceptance, not our ridicule or rejection.

Satan could not stand there, because he "does not stand in the truth." But David stood there in the center, not alone, because some of the leaders gathered around, hugging him and crying together with him. I am confident my words have not done justice to the power of the moment. We felt the presence of the Lord leading us back to biblical times and biblical ways. It was one of those situations where "you had to be there." With that in mind, read the report that our business leader/secretary wrote that night.

Hi Rich,

Here's the outcome of the biz meeting...I talked to the leaders from the Philippines and their take on this whole thing is like mine...you LIVE your walk. Your LIFE is your ministry.

Here's the info:

Role of Biz Person
1. *To be humble and pray and seek his face and turn from our wicked ways in our world [2 Chron. 7:14].*
2. *Through Marketplace Reconciliation, turn our hearts to our people, embrace them, tangibly meet their needs, and take care of the needy and social outcasts, which will produce signs and wonders.*

What We Need From the Church:
1. *Release us by standing beside us...we're in this together*
2. *Pray for us for the guts to JUST DO it!*
Love you so much,
Nancy Duarte

It is not at all what I had expected the document to look like. But it surely is what the Lord had for us that day. In fact, I think the Lord led us through this exercise to show us something of great value. There was a tremendous amount of knowledge in the room that afternoon. Powerful men and women who cared deeply about the things of God had come to seek Him. But God showed us what we could accomplish in our own wisdom...nothing.

Clearly the Lord is concerned that His kings care for the hurting, the oppressed, the disenfranchised people of our cities. There is a simple and straightforward message that we must respond to. The hurting people need the help of the kings. This is a ministry that God has anointed kings to succeed in.

More Than Money-Doling

In Acts chapter 6, where the apostles called for help in the food ministry, it was the businesspeople that they went to for help. The apostles added this thought: "It is not good for us to leave our ministry, to do this ministry" (my paraphrase). There are different callings on kings and priests. Now think about it. Most benevolent work is still done by "priestly" types, who often become very frustrated and disillusioned. It is time for the "kings" to step up and take the lead.

At the beginning of my study, I believed that the main role of the king was to bring in the provision for the endtime harvest. I still believe that is *a* major role; I just don't think it is *the* major role of the kings in the coming move of God. It does not take an Einstein to figure out that the kings are needed to bring provision; after all, most priests lack the resources. So, the kings will have to do this, but that is neither the only, nor the most important role of kingly anointing.

God@Work

We gain more insight into the role of the kings by seeing the instruction that God gave his kings in the Bible. Over and over again we see that God instructs the kings to execute judgment, justice, and righteousness. As we look at several passages, hear the Word of the Lord.

Thus says the Lord: "Go down to the house of the king of Judah, and there speak this word, and say, 'Hear the word of the Lord, O king of Judah, you who sit on the throne of David, you and your servants and your people who enter these gates! Thus says the Lord: "Execute judgment and righteousness, and deliver the plundered out of the hand of the oppressor. Do no wrong and do no violence to the stranger, the fatherless, or the widow, nor shed innocent blood in this place. For if you indeed do this thing, then shall enter the gates of this house, riding on horses and in chariots, accompanied by servants and people, kings who sit on the throne of David. But if you will not hear these words, I swear by Myself," says the Lord, "that this house shall become a desolation" ' " (Jeremiah 22:1-5).

Thus says the Lord God: "Enough, O princes of Israel! Remove violence and plundering, execute justice and righteousness, and stop dispossessing My people," says the Lord God (Ezekiel 45:9).

Blessed be the Lord your God, who delighted in you, setting you on His throne to be king for the Lord your God! Because your God has loved Israel, to establish them forever, therefore He made you king over them, to do justice and righteousness (2 Chronicles 9:8).

Blessed be the Lord your God, who delighted in you, setting you on the throne of Israel! Because the Lord has loved Israel forever, therefore He made you king, to do justice and righteousness (1 Kings 10:9).

The Lord is saying that we must remove violence and plundering and stop dispossessing His people. God is very concerned about honesty and integrity, and is calling for moral excellence and high character in the kings. In God's economy, the bottom line is not financial success, but the operation of righteousness and removal of all oppression. When Jonah went to Nineveh to proclaim the Lord's judgment on that city, the king cried out orders for an end to violence and doing evil (see Jon. 3).

As kings in the service of God today, we must begin to lift the oppression and relieve the violence under which so many in our world live. There is an oppression of poverty and an oppression of racial discrimination. There is an oppression experienced by some women in the workplace, and there is oppression brought about by one's own workaholic mentality. God is calling the kings to lift the oppression. We have often seen the church and church-related ministries as the key to lifting oppression. Many parachurch ministries have also taken up this task.

Leaders, God is giving you the power to stop the oppression. You cannot sit back and fund mercy ministries and believe that your job is complete. You must get in the game. Look around you. Opportunities abound, both in America and in developing nations around the world. I am personally a part of business initiatives that are lifting oppression and removing violence around the world. Nations such as Indonesia and numerous other developing nations and cities like Minneapolis are being touched as kings and priests join hands to make Jesus real in a hurting world. And in these cases, the kings are leading the priests![1]

I have come to understand that there will be no change in the spiritual climate over our cities without involvement in the things that touch the heart of God. The kings must become proactively involved in stopping various kinds of abuse, feeding the hungry, caring for the lonely, and generally exposing and eliminating oppression.

God's Man for the Job

In the book *Kings and Priests*, David High points to Deuteronomy 17:14-20 where we find further instruction about the role of the kings. First we learn that the kingly anointing is a God-given anointing.[2] The people were to set a king over themselves "whom the Lord your God chooses" (Deut. 17:15). Kings, like priests, must know they have heard the voice of God about their place of employment. The matter is not one iota less important for one than the other. This is a choosing of God, and we must not manipulate it, orchestrate it, plan it, or use personal power and influence to gain it. We must trust God to place us where He wants us, so that we might always have His anointing upon us.

Hosea chapter 8 tells of a time when the people set up kings, but not the ones God had chosen. Because of it, they sowed the wind, and reaped the whirlwind (see Hos. 8:7).

Kings From Among You

The second principle is that God will raise up kings from among you. I believe there is an instruction here to the kings as well as to the priests. To the kings, make sure you are in the place God has for you, but don't assume you need to change. To the priests who govern over houses full of kings, I believe there is a word of instruction for you as well. You don't need to steal kings from other places, which has always been a problem with the people of God.

God speaks here to a people who say, "Let's go get a king over there, and set up an alliance with that nation." The results in Hosea were unholy alliances. From my years of experience as a pastor, I know it is a problem in the modern Church as well. In any given city, there is continual trading (or stealing?) of church members that gives a semblance of church growth. Really this is just a movement of God's people from one congregation to another.

Pastors, please hear my heart on this one. God is calling you to raise up kings from your own body, not to covet the kings that are in other congregations. I heard the story about a pastor who was visiting the largest congregation in the world, the one in Seoul, South Korea, where Pastor Cho is the pastor. At the end of the service, the church offers the opportunity to tour the facilities and learn more about its ministry. This visiting pastor took the tour, and used it for the opportunity to ask, "How many millionaires are there in this congregation?" I do not recall the exact answer, but it was 50 or 100, or some large number. This pastor replied, "I could grow a large church also, if I had 100 millionaires." The man leading the tour said, "Oh sir, you don't understand. There were no millionaires here when Pastor Cho started; they became millionaires under his ministry."

We need to let God choose the kings, and then we need to develop them into all that God has for them.

Businesspeople and—Horses?

The Lord's next principle is even more specific. He says that the king "shall not multiply horses for himself, nor cause the people to return to Egypt to multiply horses" (Deut. 17:16). Horses were a sign of strength, a sign of power. The psalmist has written, "Some trust in chariots, and some in horses; but we will remember the name of the Lord our God" (Ps. 20:7). The message? Kings need to know that their strength and power is not in what they own. Psalm 33:17 also tells us that "a horse is a vain hope for safety."

In those days, Egypt was the source for horses. Unfortunately, Egypt is also a picture of going back to the former way of life—back to the world's ways—of seeking strength in what we had before we came to Christ. The truth is you cannot go back, and you do not need to rely on the strength and power of past events for the position that God has called you to today.

We read next that the king shall not "multiply wives for himself, lest his heart turn away; nor shall he greatly multiply silver and gold for himself (Deut. 17:17). If you will, allow me to remind you of an old teaching, one that I was given when I was just starting out as a pastor years ago. I was told to look out for three things that the enemy would use to bring me down: the girls, the gold, and the glory. That is what we have here. In other words: money, sex, and power.

Guarding Your Life

Kings and priests alike need to guard themselves carefully. Men and women alike need to heed this warning: We must guard ourselves in the area of moral purity, and from seeking power and position. In terms of possessions, we must not let them possess us, but we must determine to be good stewards of all that the Lord is giving us.

David had a major morality problem, but he learned from it, repented of it, and went on with God. If you, like David, have mis-used authority, sinned through immorality, or withheld the resources that God has entrusted to your care, that does not elim-inate you from the kingly anointing. However, you must change your ways, repent of that sin, and get your heart right with God. The time to do so is now. Let the kingly anointing and the priest-ly anointing be the anointing of purity!

Let me just go back and reinforce this again. Solomon's heart was turned from God because of his many wives, whether his prob-lem was born out of the intense sexual drive that was upon him for more and more women, or for political alliances. I speak to you men and women today: One of the downfalls of your kingly anointing may be your unfaithfulness to the Lord. This may be brought on by unfaithfulness to the one partner God has given you. Or, for those of you who are single, that unfaithfulness to the Lord may be brought on by not keeping yourself sexually pure for that one partner who comes your way. Guard yourselves.

With regard to money, the Deuteronomy passage says you shall not "*greatly* multiply silver and gold." The Bible also says, "If riches increase, do not set your heart on them" (Ps. 62:10). Rather, thank God for them, and keep your trust in the Lord.

Making a Copy of the Law

One last principle from Deuteronomy and consider this care-fully: "He shall write for himself a copy of this law in a book..." (Deut. 17:18b). He shall write for himself.

Usually the priest would have a copy of the law, and if some-one else wanted a copy, they would have to make that copy for themselves. In families, the copy would be handed down from one generation to the next; dad would hand a copy of the law to his son or daughter. But the Lord says to the king, "Dad's copy is not good enough for you. You need to copy it for yourself." It's not good enough for you to hire a secretary and send her or him to copy it. No, the kings are to copy it personally.

Avoiding the "Fat-Baby" Syndrome

Kings, you cannot rely on the priests to feed you the Word of God. It is not enough for you to say, "I'm a king, and I will do my kingly thing. I will do my business, and when I go to church, the priest will feed me." That is not good enough. The godly, anointed king will take the Word of God, and study it for himself. As verse 19 says, "...he shall read it all the days of his life, that he may learn to fear the Lord...." He will take notes, he will read the Word, and he will receive direction for himself. The businesswoman will know the Word of the Lord for herself so that what she receives is from God and not from man. She will hold God in awe.

Do you know why this is so important in these days? When the revival comes, people will stream by your desk wanting answers to spiritual questions. When they come, you need to have the answers, not because you heard a good sermon, but because you were with the Lord that morning, and He spoke out of His Word. Only then can you say, "Look what I read this morning—look what God showed me—here it is!"

No More "Better Than Thou"

Deuteronomy 17:20 adds this important concept for the kings: If the king learns to fear the Lord, and keep His words, "his heart may not be lifted above his brethren." The Lord God wants to birth humility in kings that will not allow them to set their hearts above others. The God-anointed kings will serve in humility.

Pride is the father of all sin. James 3:16 says, "For where envy and self-seeking exist, confusion and every evil thing are there." Pride is what we ride, and we ride on it so faithfully that we don't recognize the power it holds in our lives. You could call pride a PowerRide. It becomes so integrated within us, we often don't recognize the stranglehold it has on our words and actions. Pride accompanies everything we do or say. Of course, I can recognize it quicker in my wife or others than in myself. We all need people whom we will listen to when they encourage or reprove. We must let them speak to the issues of pride, which we cannot see on our own, in order to uproot the sin that God hates: pride. Remember: "For all have sinned and fall short of the glory of God" (Rom 3:23).

At the end of Deuteronomy chapter 17 we see that obedience will result in a tremendous blessing. The days of both him and his children will be prolonged. You and your whole family will live longer, healthier, safer. Do you want a blessing for your children? Get ahold of the Word of God and let it guide your life. God will bless your kingly ministry, and He will also bless your children. He'll multiply your days. He will strengthen your life. Receive God's awesome plan for you!

Wherever I go with this message to the business and professional person, I receive a similar response. They have been hearing in their heart from the Lord, but need the spiritual validation to continue on. Here is a letter I received from Brent Largent, one of God's kings in Central California.

When We Need to "Buck" the System

I am the owner of Third Millennium Media, a computer graphic design and multi-media company in Modesto. I attended the Kings and Priests Seminar last Saturday and was deeply affected by the message the Lord delivered through you. It was so freeing and validating. Since the seminar, I've been pouring over my notes and listening to your messages and with each exposure I have become convinced of the message's veracity.

Let me give you some background. After choosing to follow Christ in the summer of 1982, I discovered I had a passion and zeal for things spiritual that my peers (high school folks) did not exhibit. That zeal was interpreted by my peer pastors and by myself over the years as a clarion call to full-time priestly ministry. In other words, if you have this much interest in spiritual things, they said, obviously you are called to a priestly ministry. Thus for the next few years, I pursued a priestly path involving myself in every kind of ministry during my early college experience with a sincere desire to "go into the ministry."

In the summer of 1986 the Lord gave me a clarification of His calling. He said that the passion and zeal I exhibited was intended for kingly not priestly work. Of course, I didn't understand or use those terms then. When I announced to my pastor that I was no longer "going into the ministry," but was going to minister to lost college students by becoming a full-time history professor, it was as if I single-handedly derailed God's personal calling for my life. I was told in no uncertain terms that I was very wrong, out of God's will, and in danger of becoming a backslider. When I announced my engagement to my lovely wife, Linda, the pastor, completely convinced that she was stealing me away from ministry, boldly stated that he was praying against me. No way on earth that a teacher with my abilities could be of any heavenly use in any place other than the priestly ministry, he claimed. Well, I finished college and God provided a teaching job in a college history department. I taught there for four years and then was led to start a business in computer graphics.

Since 1993, I've been in the computer graphics business and have seen God provide in a manner I've never experienced before. My wife is also self-employed and her ministry through business is fabulous.

Throughout this time, however, I had the nagging thought that I really didn't listen to God. What my pastor had pounded into me over two years doggedly stuck with me. The enemy would use his words to discourage the career path I had taken. "You're wrong, you're out of God's will. See, you had to leave teaching. That obviously was not the will of God." And so it would go. The enemy's deception was strengthened by the fact that I received no validation from my pastors to the contrary. I remained in this vicious cycle undoubtedly hamstrung and less effective in the calling God bestowed upon me. I now realize what a clever deception that was. The words of truth you spoke broke deception's shackles and freed both my wife and my spirit.

Thank you pastor. During the seminar, my wife and I occasionally whispered to each other, "That's what we've been saying for years." Now you have given us biblical validation to confirm what we already knew in our hearts. Our businesses are our ministries. That is our calling at this time. God may change it, of course. I feel and know that I am where God wants me to be and it's okay to pursue the business calling with the same fire and vigor as a pastor would his. I am ready to turn God's business resources he has allowed my wife and me to steward over to him for the end-time harvest. Let's do it!

That is what God is doing all over the world right now. He is calling the kings into the ministry. In the Bible we read that He has made us kings and priests. We have been using those words from God's Word to speak to the reality that there is calling on everyone in the Body of Christ. The kingly anointing will lead to business and professional work. The priestly anointing will lead to church work and missionary work. But both of these are callings for the Body of Christ today...the king and the priest working together.

Praying the Workers Out of Boot Camp

One of the continuing problems we face in the church is that we have not had a paradigm for ministry in the marketplace. I thank God that is changing in these days. We need to release the entire force into the harvest. Jesus said, "The harvest truly is great, but the laborers are few; therefore pray the Lord of the harvest to send out laborers into His harvest" (Lk. 10:2).

I think we can agree that the harvest is still great today. There is no problem with a lack of "produce." The problem is that we have a shortage of workers. Yet I wonder if that really is the problem. Are we short of workers? Or are the workers available, but not released? When Jesus spoke of this in Luke chapter 10, He did not wring His hands in despair over the shortage of workers. He simply said, "Pray, and the Lord of the harvest will send the workers into the harvest." The workers were available, they were just not harvesting. Could it be that God has raised up this entire army of workers, and we have left them in boot camp instead of sending them to the front lines? When we continue to teach from the old paradigm, "Go into the ministry," instead of the new paradigm, "You are in the ministry," we support the problem more than the solution.

We have already spoken about the role of the priest in announcing revival, and the role of the king in bringing in that revival. God has spoken clearly in His Word: One of the great signs of the last days is this coming worldwide harvest. I happen to be one of those who believes the next great outpouring might have its beginning in the marketplace. Maybe it will be at your place of employment.

I will deal in the last chapter of the book with some very practical ways for you to use your kingly anointing in the marketplace, and therefore fulfill the role of the king.

Endnotes

1. Organizations that are involved in this type of ministry include: Kingdom Oil under the direction of Jay Bennett in Minneapolis, Minnesota; Indonesian Relief Fund under the direction of Paul Tan in Claremont, California; and The Nehemiah Partners led by Dennis Doyle of Eden Prairie, Minnesota.

2. David R. High, *Kings and Priests* (Oklahoma City, OK; Books for Children of the World, 1997), 20.

Chapter Seven

The Call of God

But as God has distributed to each one, as the Lord has called each one, so let him walk. And so I ordain in all the churches (1 Corinthians 7:17).

When I was only five or six years old, I knew I wanted to be a preacher. As I grew older I said things like, "I want to be a preacher and a truck driver," or "a coach and a preacher." But basically, I knew I was called to preach the gospel. Between my junior and senior years in high school, the Lord dramatically confirmed that call at a youth camp. From that moment on, I knew "I was called to preach."

I am sure my story can be repeated time after time with slightly different timings and examples. The call of God is powerful, life changing, and very real. Now, consider this question: If there is "a call to preach" or "a call to missions," is there also "a call to computer programming" or "a call to sales or carpentry"? What about the boy who wants to be a policeman? Is that just a childhood fantasy, or does God call believers into law enforcement like He does to preaching? What about the girl who says, "One day I want to own my own business"? Is that just a dream born out of some frustration that came by watching women being passed over in the marketplace? Or is that a dream that was placed in the heart by Father God, in the same way He placed it in another little girl's heart to serve Him in Africa?

Does God call individuals to serve in business and government—teaching—and dozens of other professions? Or is the "call of God" reserved for the select few who are "going into the professional ministry"? I believe the Bible clearly teaches that the "call of God" is for the entire Body of Christ.

A "Called" Craftsman

In Exodus chapter 31 there is a fascinating story about a man named Bezaleel.

According to Strong's Concordance, the name "Bezalel" means "in the shadow (or protection) of God."[1]

I believe it is no coincidence that the text says that God "called by name Bezalel" (Ex. 31:21a). When God calls something, He puts His sovereignty over it. For instance, God called the darkness "night," and He called the light "day." He is Lord over it all. When we read that God "called by name Bezalel," it does not mean that God figured out what his name was and from then on called him by name. We know that God often changes a name to fit with His purpose for the person. He changed Abram to Abraham and Sarai to Sarah. He would call Jacob, Israel, and would call Saul, Paul. So when we see that God called him Bezalel, or "the one in shadow or protection of God," it is significant. Why do I say that? Because God had either personally spoken with Bezalel about being a craftsman, or He had personally revealed the man's name to Moses. God had a purpose for this man, and would keep him in His protection to see that Bezalel could fulfill his destiny. And what was his destiny? It was to be a Spirit-filled worker in the creative arts.

> *Then the Lord spoke to Moses, saying: "See, I have called by name Bezalel...And I have filled him with the Spirit of God, in wisdom, in understanding, in knowledge, and in all manner of workmanship"* (Exodus 31:1-3).

Here, God fills with the Spirit, not just for preaching...not just for evangelizing...not just for prophesying.... God fills with the Spirit for the purpose of workmanship.

God has a special anointing for even the most difficult tasks of this high tech age. As I read this passage, I realized that God has a special anointing that will make your mind as clear as it can be, so you can receive the creative thoughts that He alone can give you. God can even make your motor skills and mind function in the way it should, so that what He wants you to accomplish will be accomplished.

For those of you in sales, God will open the door to the people who are ready to buy, and give you the right approach to make the sale. For those of you who are working at a computer, God will give you special insight. God has an anointing for marketing, manufacturing, management, and construction. He anoints some as attorneys at law and some as government workers. God can, and will, anoint you for the business at hand, the profession He has called you to. Thank God, because of Bezalel, we can see that He calls us to a variety of professions.

Many people know very little about Bezalel as a Bible character. Very few sermons are preached about him, and he doesn't even make the "Personality Profile" lists. But God called him by name. God says he chose Bezalel in order that he might "work in all manner of workmanship" (Ex. 31:5b). The Bible does not say, "all manners of ministry," nor does it say, "all manners of priestly work." He called him by name and filled him with the Spirit, in order that he might work.

The giftings that are given in this chapter are for designing artistic works of gold, silver, and bronze; for cutting jewels, carving wood, and in all manner of workmanship. I believe the Lord keeps repeating the phrase, "in all manner of workmanship," for our sakes. Our tendency would be to think God had him designing religious jewelry and building church buildings. It *was* for the purpose of building the temple. But also, it is obvious that God has sent the anointing for all kinds of workmanship.

Every gifting or anointing we have comes from the Lord. The enemy endeavors to distort the gift and turn it to his purpose—in some cases he is able to do that. However, the more we come to realize that the gifts and anointing we have are from the Lord, and that God wants us to use them in the marketplace for Him, the more likely it is that we can find fulfillment in serving God through our work.

We can see the same truth taught in First Corinthians 7:17. Paul tells us to remain in the calling in which we were called. In most cases, this text is interpreted in light of marriage, which is the context in this chapter. However, to limit that call to marriage, or to singleness, could cause you to miss the understanding of the call of God in your life. "The Lord has called each one." There is a call for you and it is from God. He has a plan for you, a destiny for you to fulfill.

You don't have to change professions when you become a Christian; you don't need to leave your job into order to "go into the ministry." God is calling you and will anoint you for His purposes right where you are—not just to fund this revival, but to be on the front lines in bringing in the harvest.

Tuning in to God's Call

Even though I knew from a young age that I was called to be a pastor, the same was not true for my son or my daughter. Of course, both our children were raised in a pastor's home, and were asked the question through the growing-up years: "Are you going into the ministry?" Both our children love the Lord deeply and are raising their children in a godly environment, but neither of them is following in our professional footsteps. And I am very thankful for the fact that they have heard from the Lord and know that they can serve Him in the marketplace.

Our son walked away from the Lord for a few years. There was such intensity in his return that it seemed natural for him to serve on our church staff as an associate minister. He became very effective and fulfilled an important role in our congregation, but that was not his call. Now that he is operating in the "kingly anointing," he and his wife know that God has a place for him in the marketplace. In terms of spiritual effectiveness, I know it will allow him to far exceed what he could have achieved in a church setting.

Our daughter and her husband also find their role best fulfilled in the marketplace setting. I love to hear our children talking about the ministry of the marketplace, to see the anointing on their lives for this calling. I know they will be a part of the coming revival.

What is required before God will call you? When Abraham was called, he obeyed by faith (see Heb. 11:8). I believe that God is stirring up faith in some of you readers right now to help you obey. Moses was called to lead a people who had rejected him. They said of him, "Who made you a ruler and a judge?" (Acts 7:35a) Well, in this case, God had. If you will listen closely to the voice of God, you will be able to discern His call for your life. It may not be into the most natural or easy arenas. He may even call you to lead people who don't want to be led, and you may need to learn the lessons of patience that Moses learned. (Maybe that's how Moses became the humblest man on earth [see Num. 12:3].) Aaron was called to assist Moses (see Ex. 4:16), and we must learn, likewise, that there are times when God may call you to serve another, to assist in the fulfillment of someone else's dream.

When the Lord called Gideon, He used the words, "The Lord is with you, you mighty man of valor!" (Judg. 6:12b; see also Judg. 6:11-16). Gideon responded by asking why everything was going wrong. "Where are all the miracles?" he asked. He described himself as from the weakest clan, the least important in his father's house—not necessarily the best self-image for a man destined to lead the army of God. But as with Gideon, so it is with you. Have you ever felt like Gideon? God is looking on the person that He knows you can be. He can work in your life in spite of your current doubts. When He calls you, it is not because of what you have done, but because of what He can do with you.

The prophet Amos was a sheepherder when God called him. "I was no prophet, nor was I a son of a prophet, but...the Lord said to me, 'Go, prophesy to My people Israel' " (Amos 7:14b-15).

God is looking for people who will neither rely on, nor blame their past, but will willingly respond to the call of God. Some don't. One rich man in the Bible was called to follow the Lord, and yet he was held captive to his possessions and was unwilling to pay the price to follow the Lord (see Mk. 10:21-22).

The Lord is calling again, and that call is for you as surely as it is for me. The plan of God is for a revival of such major proportions that all will hear the good news of Jesus, and He will pour out His Spirit on all flesh. To bring in that kind of harvest, we need workers in all sectors of society. For many people, maybe even the majority, more time is spent at work than any other place. It would follow that, in the wisdom of God, He would call workers into the marketplace.

Whether it is Bezalel or Paul, the Word of God is clear; He is calling. He called Abraham, Moses, Aaron, Gideon, Amos, and the rich young ruler. Now He is calling you!

Endnote

1. James Strong, *Strong's Exhaustive Concordance of the Bible* (Peabody, MA: Hendrickson Publishers, n.d.), **Bezalel** (#1212).

Chapter Eight

The Power of Obedience

Oh, that they had such a heart in them that they would fear Me and always keep all My commandments, that it might be well with them and with their children forever! (Deuteronomy 5:29)

Obeying the "Little Things" Means a Lot

Every day things happen around us that have an impact on our lives, but we often do not know the full ramification of these things as they happen. The truth is, many opportunities to receive the full blessing of the Lord are missed because of our disobedience. I was with a man one time who apparently heard God's voice on a very regular basis.

We had just walked into a restaurant, and on the way in, I noticed that he had stopped at a table and said something like, "God bless you" to the couple seated there. He asked me if I had seen him stop at the table, and when I affirmed I had, he told me, "The Lord whispered to me to speak a blessing over that couple. If I had not been obedient in that command, how could I expect Him to give me a command of greater impact?" I asked him the question, "What is the most important thing you have heard from the Lord?" He answered, "The last thing." He went on to explain the importance of hearing and obeying in the seemingly small things; for why would God entrust us with big things, if we are not willing to obey the small things?

Do you understand what I am saying? If you will not listen to the last thing—big or small, strange or normal, within or outside of your comfort zone—why should you think He will direct you when you ask for help with your business? Oh, there is no doubt He wants to bless you and your work, but He is looking for obedience. The Bible is full of mandates similar to this one:

> *Observe and obey all these words which I command you, that it may go well with you and your children after you forever, when you do what is good and right in the sight of the Lord your God* (Deuteronomy 12:28).

A friend of mine in a major Midwest city tells an amazing story. Even though he was the owner/operator of his business, he felt the Lord was prompting him to go to Bible college. The classes met every day from 8:00 a.m. to 12 noon. Know that this would impact his ability to practice his profession, he determined to be obedient to the Lord and enrolled in the college. He was quite surprised when, after only three months in college, his business had doubled—yes, *doubled*, even though he was only working half time. He then states that in one year the business had tripled and by the time he had finished the two-year course in Bible college, the business had quadrupled.

Who would think that cutting your work time back to one half would cause your business to grow four times? In the natural that kind of thing would not happen. But when the Lord calls for obedience and you obey, then He is able to make it so that things go well with you and with your children forever.

My friend said that his business is in the top 1 percent of businesses in his field in the USA, and that when he goes to conventions many want to talk to him about how his business has grown. The answer he is able to give is that God has done this. What a powerful testimony!

I am not recommending that cutting back your office hours is the latest technique for business growth. What I am recommending is that it is wise to obey the Lord in all the things He asks of you. Oftentimes, you will have no understanding of the outcome, and some of the commands might even seem like wasted time or unfruitful effort. But I have seen the effects of obedience enough times, both in the Bible and in life, to know the principle is absolutely true.

Go to Guatemala?

Let me take a few moments to trace the progression of some of the revelation I have received about kings and priests. As I think back on this now, I realize that one of the key components was my own obedience to a word I received during a conference in Argentina in October 1996.

Omar Cabrera was preaching on healing at the annual Harvest Evangelism International Institute. It was a good message and I was listening closely, because I respect this man so much, and wanted to learn all that I could. As I sat there, suddenly I heard as clearly as I can ever remember hearing, the voice of the Lord ask me, "Rich, are you willing to go to Guatemala?" My mind was not on Guatemala, and I knew no one from Guatemala. I knew Guatemala was in Central America, but I did not know where. My point is, this word from the Lord came out of the blue. Nevertheless, it was so clear that I wrote it down in my notebook, and even dated and timed it: "3:56 p.m., October 30, 1996."

Jack Deere, a friend of mine, often says, "The all-knowing God does not ask questions in order to gain information." I knew that was the case here. God was not asking a question that I was to answer; He was giving a command that I was to obey.

As I walked out of that session, a young girl tapped me on the shoulder. When I turned around, she asked me if I was from the United States. Upon hearing my answer, she asked me if I would forgive her for the feeling she had against my country, especially for the way we had treated her country. I assured her of my forgiveness and asked where she was from. You guessed it, Guatemala.

This was my chance! Already God was giving me an open door into this nation or at least that is what I thought. I asked her, if I were to come to her country, could we do this identificational repentance on a larger scale? She told me she no longer lived there, but could introduce me to her pastor, Harold Caballeros. I soon made arrangements to meet Pastor Harold, and before the year was out, Wilma and I were in Guatemala. We have since returned many times, and now have Guatemalans whom we count among our very closest friends. This message to kings and priests was to have its birth out of that word about Guatemala.

We discovered in Guatemala a quiet but powerful revival. Conservative estimates conclude that the nation is now over 45 percent born-again Christians. The church Pastor Caballeros leads, El Shaddai, has been seeing between 200 and 250 converts to Christ every week—for over three years. Harold and his wife, Cecelia, are gifted not only in the nation they live in, but also have been raised up by God for a powerful international ministry. Throughout the Spanish and English-speaking worlds, God has anointed Harold with a life-giving message.

That March we invited Pastor Caballeros to our congregation in California, and on that Sunday, before he preached, he prophesied over our congregation. Part of that word included this: "You are pregnant with a vision that will change the ministry of this house. Your pregnancy will be birthed by December and will affect the nations of the world by the spirit." As my wife wrote this in the margin of her Bible, she added the text he referred to—Luke 1:26. I had forgotten that reference by the December morning in 1997 when the Lord gave me the revelation that would revolutionize my ministry—about kings and priests. Of course, Luke 1:26 is the start of the passage about the birth of Jesus. That is what the Lord would use to show me the difference today between the roles of kings and priests.

Could it be that the Lord would ask a seemingly totally unrelated question about going to Guatemala—in order to find out if I would obey—before He gave the word about kings and priests? It would appear so! Obedience in the small things opens the door for deeper revelation, and the privilege of being obedient in greater things. I cannot begin to imagine where the Lord will lead next, as I realize I have only seen the tip of the iceberg of all the revelation that He has to give. One thing we need to remember about God is that He always has more to give—more revelation, more peace, more grace, more resources. He will never run out.

Lessons From History

If we are going to walk as kings in the Kingdom, then we must learn our lessons from the kings of the Bible. When the kings did what was good and right in the eyes of the Lord God, they prospered.

In First Kings chapter 15 we encounter the story of King Asa, who did right in the eyes of the Lord. For years he had walked with God in obedience before getting off track later in life. Even then, his sin was not so much deliberate disobedience as choosing the easy way, rather than the right way. King Asa was informed by Azariah, "The Lord is with you while you are with Him. If you seek Him, He will be found by you; but if you forsake Him, He will forsake you" (2 Chron. 15:2b).

We see that King Asa's heart was fully committed to the Lord all the days of his life. There are so many bad kings, it is refreshing to look at some of the good kings like Asa and David.

Before considering the life of David, let us recall that in First Samuel chapter 8 the people demanded a king. They were unsatisfied with just having God as their king. "We want to be like the other nations, and we want a king." This displeased the prophet Samuel, and he talked to the Lord about it. But the Lord told him to heed the word of the people, and to remember that they had not rejected Samuel but they had rejected the Lord (see 1 Sam. 8:7).

Obedience Is Better Than Sacrifice

In chapter 9 the Lord anointed Saul as the first king. Saul began with a strong anointing from God. He was a man of God, selected by God for this time. He demonstrated God's strength in his life. As we read about Saul, we find that he did some awesome things. Among other deeds, his speech at his coronation was glorious to the Lord. However, it wasn't very long in Saul's life before he lost his anointing as king, and became disobedient.

I encourage you to read this for yourself, because the Lord is concerned about very specific obedience. God can give a word to you, and even though you do most of it, if you do not do all of it, you may lose the Lord's blessing. That is what happened to Saul. He did a lot of what God had instructed him, but he did not complete all that the Lord had for him to do.

Later the Lord said to Samuel, "I greatly regret that I have set up Saul as king, for he has turned back from following Me, and has not performed My commandments" (1 Sam. 15:11a). As you read this text, you discover that God was grieved for having appointed Saul as king. He would, in fact, depose him because he had not completely obeyed the Lord.

Samuel reminded Saul that God had made him king even though, in his own right, he was small (see 1 Sam. 15:17). It will do well for us to be continually reminded that God has made us king, and that the kingship we walk in demands full obedience. A few verses later, Samuel went to Saul and asked, "What are you doing?" Saul made up a story—a story that was about 80-90 percent truth and about 10-20 percent false—to make himself look good. He wanted it to look as if he were honoring God. The Lord had told him to completely destroy the wicked Amalekites and to wipe them out. When Samuel confronted him, Saul replied that he had obeyed the Lord. As Samuel asked him then about keeping the best for himself, even though the Lord had said to destroy it all, his answer was, "Oh, we kept it to make sacrifice to the Lord" (see 1 Sam. 15:18-21). It was a very "religious" kind of language; unfortunately a language still in use today.

It was in this context that Samuel spoke the classic words, "To obey is better than sacrifice" (1 Sam. 15:22b). Consider again the conversation between Samuel and Saul.

"Why didn't you destroy it?"

"Oh, because I was keeping it so that I could make a sacrifice."

"Listen Saul, it is better for you to obey than to sacrifice."

You cannot just live your life the way you want to, going your own way, disobedient to God, and believe that you can walk into church on Sunday, make a sacrifice to the Lord, and everything will be all right.

Hear me well! Salvation is a free gift from God. Hallelujah! We can thank Him that we live in the day of grace. But many of us have tried to buy our way back, instead of living the life of obedience. Read and comprehend the Word of the Lord to Saul and to us, through Samuel:

> ... *"Has the Lord as great delight in burnt offerings and sacrifices, as in obeying the voice of the Lord? Behold, to obey is better than sacrifice, and to heed than the fat of rams. For rebellion is as the sin of witchcraft, and stubbornness is as iniquity and idolatry. Because you have rejected the word of the Lord, He also has rejected you from being king"* (1 Samuel 15:22-23).

From that moment on, even though he would remain king in the natural realm, Saul lost the anointing from God to be the king. It was because of rebellion. This set the stage for the Lord to anoint David as king.

An Obedient King

The Lord had told Samuel not to mourn, for He would provide a king from the house of Jesse (see 1 Sam. 16:1). So, they brought in all of Jesse's sons, and as you may recall, David, the youngest son, did not even make the lineup. However, with the reminder that man looks on the outward appearance but the Lord looks on the heart, the Lord led Samuel to reject all the older brothers (see 1 Sam. 16:7). When David came in, the Lord said, "Arise, anoint him; for this is the one!" (1 Sam. 16:12) David became king, while Saul still reigned on the throne. From that day on, the spirit of the Lord came upon David with power.

This period in David's life is very important for us to understand. Right now many of you are where David was. God has called you, reached out to you, laid His hand on you. But no one else knows it—only you and God. Let us learn some lessons from David and allow the Holy Spirit to minister to us as we read. The story of David in First Samuel can help us to measure up to our kingly calling.

David was just a young man, a shepherd boy. After his anointing, he was immediately called to the aid of King Saul. Saul's problem was, since the spirit of the Lord had departed from him, a distressing spirit had come. He wanted to be free of this, and upon hearing that harp music would help, he said, "Find someone who plays well and bring him to me" (see 1 Sam. 16:16-17). David was the harp player of choice; we can see why by this description of him: "Look, I have seen a son of Jesse the Bethlehemite, who is skillful in playing, a mighty man of valor, a man of war, prudent in speech, and a handsome person; and the Lord is with him" (1 Sam. 16:18b).

Wow! What an awesome young man! Yes, he was awesome as described, but earlier in the same day, he was so inconspicuous that David's father would not even bring him in to be considered as king. You have to understand that what the Book of Samuel is describing here is not what you see in the natural. Remember, the Lord had said he did not look on the outward appearance, but on the heart.

If a person could have really looked at David's heart, this is what they would have seen: "a man of war"—but he had not yet fought any wars; "a mighty man of valor"—but he was just a young man. However, God was calling him and was with him. Please receive this into your spirit. Even though David knew he would sit on Saul's throne, his heart went with love and submission. This is the first step in preparation for kingship. If you would be king, learn to serve another man's vision. "If you have not been faithful in what is another man's, who will give you what is your own?" (Lk. 16:12) If you would be king, learn to serve; learn the fine art of humility. David became Saul's armor bearer.

Let God Do the Promoting

I can imagine some of us might have walked into this situation and said something like this: "Hey Saul, the reason you've got this distressing spirit is because the spirit of God has departed from you. You were disobedient, and because of it He has called for a new king. I'm the man! Step down. I'll take it from here." That was not in the spirit of David. Watch closely how young David responded to his "boss," who had become wicked in all his ways.

David played his harp for Saul, and every time he did, deliverance came. David also served as his armor bearer, but continued to fulfill his role as shepherd as well. Even though he had been anointed as king, and had favor with the sitting king, he still fulfilled his first job description. And it was in the setting as a shepherd that David was called to battle against Goliath.

This victory began to gain considerable notoriety for David, and the women danced and sang out, "Saul has slain his thousands, and David his ten thousands" (1 Sam. 18:7b). David had not yet slain ten thousand, but they were so enamored, that they began to lift him up and honor him. The king's response? "Saul was very angry, and the saying displeased him" (1 Sam. 18:8a). In modern English, he was really ticked off with the whole thing.

Nevertheless, the Bible says, "David behaved wisely in all his ways, and the Lord was with him" (1 Sam. 18:14). Even though the people were lifting him up and honoring him, even though the king was becoming upset with him, David stayed humble in his heart, true to his calling. He kept his humility, and refused to force his way. He behaved wisely. God help us develop this quality today. Knowing that the Lord has called you as king does not give you the right to force your way into positions of status or promotion. Leave that to the Lord; He knows quite well when and how to promote you.

Facing Attacks With Humility

From that day on, David fell out of favor with Saul, and Saul eyed him with evil intent and suspicion. In fact, he began plotting to take David's life. On two occasions he tried to harpoon David to the wall. Another ploy was to offer one of his daughters as David's wife—not because he wanted him as a son-in-law, but because he wanted him to battle the Philistines. He asked for no dowry, instead requesting that David slay 100 Philistines. Surely he would die in this attempt, Saul reasoned. Instead, amazingly,

David slew 200 Philistines. When that did not work, Saul had other plans for young David.

Even though Saul continued to plot the death of David, David and Saul's son Jonathan became very good friends. One day at Jonathan's urging, Saul swore to his son, "As the Lord lives, he shall not be killed" (1 Sam. 19:6b). So, David came back to Saul as in the past. But as David played the harp, Saul tried to kill him once again. Even as he ministered deliverance to the king, David had to dodge a spear and run for his life.

By this time, Saul had not only encouraged others to kill David, but he had tried several times himself to kill this godly young king (see 1 Sam. 19). One has to ask the question: "When will David turn and battle the king? When will he turn on him?" The fact is, he never will.

First Samuel chapter 24 gives a fascinating account of a particular time Saul was seeking David to kill him. Saul had gone into a cave to relieve himself, and it happened to be the very cave where David was hiding. This was David's chance to stop Saul's constant attacks on his life. But instead of taking advantage of what looked like a great opportunity, he cut off a piece of Saul's garment and said to his men, "The Lord forbid that I should do this thing to my master, the Lord's anointed, to stretch out my hand against him, seeing he is the anointed of the Lord" (1 Sam. 24:6).

Romans 13:1 teaches us that everyone who has been placed in authority has been placed there by God Almighty. Some might say, "How could someone so wicked be placed in authority by God?" Well, David was looking at Saul knowing that Saul was no longer following the call of God, yet he refused to kill Saul.

In both the church and the business community I've watched people respond exactly the opposite of David. In the Church, for instance, I've seen the Lord's anointed rejected because there was disagreement over one or two issues. People would say, "I'm going somewhere else; I'm not going to submit to you." While I have not seen anyone pick up a spear and try to kill someone in the Church, I have witnessed verbal assassination many times. I have seen people flee from godly leadership, and rise in opposition to the authority set in place by God.

I've seen the same thing in business. People have come to me and have told me that their boss, or the owner of the company, is bad and they are going to leave. They have risen up in rebellion, and have left the company at the wrong time, with the wrong motive, and with the wrong purpose.

We are in the process of training here. We are training for kingship, and David is the best example available. David would not strike back. Even when Saul finally died David's attitude remained the same (see 2 Sam. 1). One man claimed to have assisted in Saul's suicide. My paraphrase is: "He [Saul] asked me to drive the spear in his heart and I did it," but David's response was, "How was it you were not afraid...to destroy the Lord's anointed?" (see 2 Sam. 1:9-10,14).

So how are you doing in your preparation for kingly positioning? Maybe God has anointed you as king and no one else knows it. Nobody in your family knows it. Nobody in your neighborhood knows it. Nobody at work knows it. You're still just a shepherd boy. Or maybe everyone recognizes the anointing of the king on your life, and you are lifted up in every situation. How are you doing? When rebellion raises its ugly head, or when pride begins to reign, the Lord will quietly minister to you through the life of King David.

As you study the life of David, you will find that he was the most awesome king that God ever had. The other kings were measured by the life and reign of King David. Of the other kings it was said: "They did or did not do as King David had done." David learned his role from the Lord, but he prepared for his role under the most wicked of them all.

It is likely that you have seen some of the errors of your past as we have considered the preparation of David for kingship. It is time to ask the Lord for His grace. In the same way that David was able to bring peace to Saul by playing his harp, the Lord can bring that peace to you. Saul became distressed when he was under conviction. Maybe you are under conviction right now. Conviction is a good thing. Unlike guilt, which makes us feel our failure and increases our doubt that we can ever become victorious, conviction leads us to the Lord who can change us and cause us to be victorious. When the conviction comes from the Lord, we need to let it do its work. Holy Spirit, prepare us for the role you have for us.

Chapter Nine

Equipping the Kings

For the weapons of our warfare are not carnal but mighty in God for pulling down strongholds (2 Corinthians 10:4).

Years ago, as a young man just getting started in ministry, I learned a very valuable lesson about the "weapons of our warfare." I walked into my office for an appointment with a man just a few years younger than me. His mother wanted me to talk to him, and it was obvious that she was more excited about the appointment than he was. During our conversation, I said something that upset him enough that he went ballistic. He jumped to his feet, lifting my desk as he did so, throwing it over into my lap. He shouted something like this, "I am satan, and I am going to kill you." By this time my office was in a shambles, with the desk and all of its contents on the floor. But he wasn't done. He picked up a chair, and with it in throwing position over his head, he started for me as I backed up against the wall. I told him to stop, but that did no good, and he continued coming. Then I said these words, "Stop, in the name of the Lord Jesus." When I said those words, he immediately stopped. I then asked him to put the chair down, but he refused. So I tried it again, "In the name of Jesus, put the chair down." Not only did he put the chair down, but as it was over his head, he pulled it down onto himself until he was flat on the floor under the chair. The situation ended positively, and the young man later became a Christian and received deliverance from his oppression.

The evening of the "attack," as I was driving home from my office, I suddenly realized what had happened—and what had almost happened—but had been stopped by the power of Jesus' name.

I discovered what a powerful weapon we have in the name of Jesus. My words had meant nothing with my own power, but given the name of Jesus, they became "mighty in God for pulling down strongholds" (2 Cor. 10:4b).

Bringing Your Firstfruits

That afternoon, the Lord had led me into battle and had placed a weapon for victory in my hand, but I was not aware I had it until I used it. In the same way, the Lord has placed weapons in the hands of His kings that are largely unknown and unused. One of these weapons is referred to in the Bible as "firstfruits."

I need to make sure we understand that the teaching about firstfruits is for the Church. Many have viewed this principle from the Old Testament as one with no relevance for today. However, the New Testament affirms this principle, using even the Resurrection of Jesus as an example of firstfruits (see 1 Cor. 15:20). In that context we understand firstfruits like this: Since Jesus enjoyed the power of resurrection, then we can also. His resurrection is a firstfruits promise of what is to come for us.

And there is even more to this powerful principle as we look deeper into it. Paul tells us, for instance, that the firstfruits affect all the rest. "For if the firstfruit is holy, the lump is also holy" (Rom. 11:16a).

I was reminded of the power of the firstfruits in the business context as I listened in on a conversation between a couple of businessmen one day. As one businessman told the other of his vision for a creative banking venture, the second man said, "You understand that your idea is a firstfruits idea. That means that it is destined to bring destruction to the evil and worldly financial system, and also that you can touch none of it." I'm not sure what this businessman understood of that, because he has since given up the idea. But I know what I heard, and it deeply impacted me.

My mind went immediately to the passage of scripture in Joshua chapters 6 and 7 where the Israelites were entering the Promised Land, both to possess it and take it back for the Kingdom of God. As they went into the first city, Jericho, God instructed them that they could keep none of the bronze, iron, silver or gold. He called these things both the "consecrated things" and the "accursed things" (see Josh. 6: 18-19). The same things were both "consecrated" to God, if meant to be used for His kingdom purposes. However, if the people kept it for themselves, it became the "accursed thing." In the hands of God, the "consecrated" things would bring destruction in the enemies' camp. In the hands of the people, the destruction would still come, but not on the enemies' camp, rather in their own households. You may recall that the Israelites enjoyed a great victory at Jericho, and yet were soundly defeated at the much smaller city of Ai. Why? Because one man had taken the "accursed things."

As I heard this conversation in a business setting, I began to see the power of the firstfruits in the hands of the business leaders. When God gives a firstfruit, it is very important that it is used in the right manner. Properly used, this firstfruit has the power to destroy the work of the enemy. Improperly used, that is, kept in the hands of the individual, the firstfruits will bring destruction upon his own business or family.

Exactly what is a firstfruit? In Jericho it was the gold and silver from the first city that the Israelites reclaimed for God. If it were sanctified, then all of the rest would also be sanctified. But since one man failed to keep the command of God, the "curse" came upon the Israelites, and they suffered defeat.

From this we know that a "firstfruit" is a thing that comes as the first of a new kind of activity. In the Bible, the first-born animal was to be considered a firstfruit (see Ex. 13:12; Num. 3:12). I believe the kings of today can ask the Lord about firstfruits, and get His direction on the specific things that might be considered as such. As I see it, these might include: For those receiving a raise in pay, the portion of money that is the raise on the first paycheck would be a firstfruit. For a salesman with a new product, the first sale would be a firstfruit. As an author, the first commission check would be considered a firstfruit. Do you begin to see the idea here?

God is giving firstfruit weapons into the hands of His kings regularly. They are intended to bring about a change in the business community by destroying the works of the enemy, and stopping violence and oppression. When these weapons are properly administrated, God will have His way in the marketplace. Of course, there is a flip side. If we are unfaithful with the firstfruit, it has the power to bring destruction in our own lives. When unexpected and unexplained reversals come, it would be wise to revisit the principle of the firstfruits.

This a particularly powerful weapon in the hands of business and professional leaders today. The power to accomplish much of what God wants to do, in and through the kings, is available in the firstfruits. The Bible tells us more about firstfruits: They are demanded by God; they are to be the best of their kind; and they are holy to the Lord. We are not to touch these things because they are purposed for destruction—the destruction of violence and oppression often plaguing our land.

Firstfruits and You

"What am I supposed to do with the firstfruits?" In Scripture they were allotted to the priests, and they continue to provide another area where the king and the priest must work together. When the Lord blesses a king with a firstfruit, and it is given to the priest, the biblical order is in place. This will sharpen the weapon and allow it to do its most effective work in the Kingdom.

Can you begin to see what the Lord is about to do? As He brings the kings and priests together, with the weapon of first-fruits, violence and oppression can be thrown off the land. When the firstfruit is made holy, then all that follows is holy as well. God will put His hand on your finances and bring about a blessing that only He can bring. This gives you the power to battle against poverty. It is time for the kings of the Lord to stand up and be counted.

We should be hearing something like this: "As the kings of the Lord, we will work together to change the spiritual climate over our land with regard to housing the poor; we will provide jobs for the unemployed; the economy is in our hands." The kings can even bring about change with regard to the environment.

Firstfruits Versus the Tithe

Many have confused firstfruits with the tithe, and therefore believe that if they are tithing, they are operating under the principle of firstfruits. I believe the tithe and firstfruits offerings are different. A tithe is a tenth, or ten percent. You cannot give a tithe unless you know what one-tenth of the whole is. Say, for instance, that a rancher wants to tithe from his cattle. He will count them off: one, two, three, four, five, six, seven, eight, nine, and now, number ten—that is his tithe. But this is not a firstfruit, because instead of giving the first cow, he gives the last one. That is the way tithing works. You give ten percent of the whole in order to tithe, but you might give the first calf, or first check from a new salary as a firstfruits offering. We need to be faithful to the Lord with both our tithes and firstfruits. By doing so, we will have the needed weapons to win the battle—even though these have been hidden for many years. Now that you understand the weapon of firstfruits, use it for the glory of the Lord.

Defeating the Enemy—Through Blessing Others

Another powerful and often unused weapon is shown us in Luke chapter 10. Here we find the Lord sending out 70 of his servants "as lambs among wolves." The Lord sees us as lambs, and we need to act like that. I am sure that there have been times when you felt like a lamb in the presence of wolves. The weapons you carry are not intended for the destruction of people, but for the destruction of the enemy and his plans.

The weapon we speak of is the weapon of blessing. As the Lord sent out the 70, reminding them that they were lambs among wolves, He told them to first say, "Peace to this house" (Lk. 10:5b).

Speaking peace is the same as blessing. When you speak a word of blessing over someone, you are speaking the words that can bring alive God's purposes for him. Blessing words are words like these: health, prosperity, victory, God's favor, joy, and happiness. When you speak these words, they actually become weapons in your hands; not weapons against the person, but against the devil.

Overcoming Curses by Blessing

Oddly, blessing is a weapon that is intended to bring destruction—of evil words (see Lk. 6:28). Blessings can destroy the curses that have been spoken over your life or over the life of another. A curse is the opposite of a blessing. While the blessing has a positive impact, the curse has a negative impact. Often curses are spoken carelessly without thought given to the impact. Sometimes parents have spoken curses over their children: "You will never amount to much"; bosses over their employees: "You can't do anything right"; husbands or wives over their partners: "You never listen," or "You always lose things." These words, even though they might seem harmless on the surface, have a tremendous amount of negative impact and power.

The way to destroy a curse is through blessing. This weapon is greatly ignored in the marketplace. When kings begin to offer blessings on their associates, employees, customers, and competitors, the power of the curses can be broken, and the blessings will flow freely.

A friend of mine realized that his company had wronged a competitor. He went to the competitor and offered to make it right; he even offered to pay to rectify the problem. They were so impressed (shocked?) by his response, they said no remuneration was necessary. Then they actually began to do business together. There is great power in blessing. It is a weapon God has designed for the marketplace. Use it.

Authority as a Spiritual Weapon

I spoke in Chapter Four about the authority that comes to a business leader when God blesses the business with financial increase. We need to understand that the authority God gives is another weapon in the marketplace.

There are social issues facing our land that can be answered through kings operating with godly authority. We have spoken about the role of the kings in executing judgment and righteousness, and stopping oppression. The prophet Jeremiah includes the mandate that the kings are to stop innocent blood from being shed. The abortion issue is one of those where the kings need to carefully consider their role in stopping this abomination. The Lord says that if you stop the shedding of innocent blood, you can be "kings who sit on the throne of David" (Jer. 22:4b). If you do not do this, your house will become desolate. The authority God has given you is a weapon to enable you to fulfill His purposes, and bring about His destiny in your life. Use your authority as a weapon for Him.

Help Is at Hand

It is time for a new paradigm in the ministry. For one thing, we need to raise our vision higher than the local church, and start targeting entire cities for Christ. The king's involvement in this allows him or her to begin to see the harvest as God Himself pictured it for us: as "truly great" (see Lk. 10:2).

Another shift that must occur is priests must release and equip the kings into the ministry of the marketplace. They must be connected with people like Bill Hamon of Christian International Ministries Network. Bill writes, "Over the past 25 years I have heard the Holy Spirit expressing to me Christ's desire to empower God's businesspeople to become Ministers in the Marketplace."[1] I thank

God for the pioneering Bill has done in this area. He now operates the Christian International Business Network, which he founded to teach, train, equip, and activate members of the Body of Christ who are called to be ministers in the marketplace. For over eight years, Mike and Cindy Jacobs, through their ministry at Generals of Intercession, have developed conferences on "Spiritual Warfare in the Workplace." Mike is becoming a strong leader, with his anointed insight in the realm of business. Cindy offers a prophetic gift that can help clarify God's direction. These early conferences have been a spark for the fire that is starting today.

Dr. C. Peter Wagner has recently started the Wagner Leadership Institute to "train and equip men and women for leadership positions in local churches and translocal ministries."[2] Dr. Wagner has been a long-time leader in the church growth movement, the prayer movement, and the spiritual warfare and intercession movement. In this new educational approach, Dr. Wagner has added an emphasis in Marketplace Ministries.

This is exciting news for the kings who desire training to fulfill the mandate to "make your business your ministry." I am the coordinator for that track, and can assure you there will be high-level instructors to assist in the training and equipping. Having the Marketplace Ministries focus in an institution of this kind is very much on the cutting edge of what God is doing these days. A recent letter from Jack Systema, the registrar for the Institute, says that *Marketplace Ministries* seems to be the new buzz word in Christianity. Apparently, the word is getting out about the importance of such ministry preparation for the coming revival.

Having been a tenured seminary professor has uniquely equipped Dr. Wagner for the educational environment, but he sees this new Institute as considerably different from traditional models of ministerial or ordination-track education. The new method of training, which follows patterns of contemporary adult education, is not based on typical classroom education, which is programmed to meet predetermined academic standards. Instead, it incorporates a variety of labs and experiences offered as the basis for earning "training units." Training units accumulate as each student moves from one level to the next toward ministry diplomas. Wagner Leadership Institute focuses more on *impartation* than on *information*. This is not to deny the importance of information, but to note that information will be provided with the goal of imparting skills and anointing for practical ministry. Students will learn both to listen to the Holy Spirit and to interpret the Scriptures.

Another organization, Harvest Evangelism, has also added a business track to their city-reacher schools and their annual international institute in Argentina. Harvest wants to help facilitate marketplace ministries in many cities across America and in other nations of the world. This cutting-edge mission is also seeing the need to add the marketplace ministry track as a key component in reaching entire cities for God.

Both pastors and business leaders show a tremendous interest in finding help for equipping those outside the walls and organization of the local church for ministry. Marketplace ministries are coming into the mainstream of Christianity.

A new ministry aimed at the marketplace is "The Nehemiah Partners." The mission statement of this group is "Echoing God's call, and partnering with others to rebuild the biblical walls of commerce globally."[3]

God is sending out a call to business and professional leaders in the marketplace whom He has strategically trained, mentored, and placed in positions of influence in society, not for their own purposes, but for His. They are similar to Gideon's army, a select group who knows that there is more to life than business alone. Their business is their ministry. "Therefore, whether you eat or drink, or whatever you do, do all to the glory of God" (1 Cor. 10:31).

Even though The Nehemiah Partners is new and still in the formation stage, every gathering has been larger than the organizers planned for. In several American and Asian cities they have found a broad interest within the business community for help in bringing training and equipping in biblical patterns for commerce. Already they have invitations from every continent in the world to hold one of their "strategic business consultations." Apparently there are many "Nehemiah Partners" out there.

I met with some other business leaders who desired to impact the world. That day we wrote this statement: "We exist to open a wide door for a demonstration of the gospel of the Kingdom through extravagant humanitarian aid and significant business engagements in developing nations." Here are a group of kings and priests together who want to make an impact in developing nations, primarily by using business to open the door. They believe that assisting with business start-ups and strategically giving humanitarian aid can open the door for the gospel. They are not preachers or evangelists doing crusades, but assuredly the gospel will penetrate these nations because of their efforts.

A Detroit ministry, "Workplace Wisdom," has developed a web site for Christian business and professional leaders to receive both information and training. Click on at http://www.wowi.net. This same group offers a daily marketplace meditation authored by Os Hillman entitled *TGIF: Today God Is First*.

These new opportunities for training in the marketplace are opening up at the same time that God is accelerating His call for the kings to step into their destiny. The phrase, "Your business is your ministry" is becoming everyday terminology, where a couple of years ago, you would have heard it only sporadically.

Local church congregations are also stepping into the marketplace ministry stream. I am hearing occasional reports about staff pastors whose main ministry is focused on the business community, and frequent reports of more equipping and releasing ministries for business leaders in the local church. Greater Works Outreach, a church in Pittsburgh, Pennsylvania, by the way, hosts a weekly ministry to the business community and provides a senior staff pastor to lead in that dynamic ministry.

The congregation that Wilma and I serve in Sunnyvale, California is also providing a new paradigm in this realm. When it became obvious that the Lord was giving us a message that needed to be shared in a broader context than our local church, the members sent us out with their blessing and their support. Under the old paradigm, we would have resigned our position with the church, entered into a time of fund-raising, and then would be able to take the message out to the Church at large. The process would have taken several months, and this urgent message would have been delayed.

Instead, we were able to accomplish the entire process in just a few weeks. We opened the doors of this ministry in 1992, and from the very inception have carried a vision that encompassed more than the local church. That foundation of caring for the whole Body of Christ enabled us to move rapidly at the end of 1998 and early 1999. The other key was the anointed and gifted staff whom the Lord had brought to the church during her first seven years. There was no need to look for a senior pastor, as Scott and Janet Abke had been serving as copastors for a number of years and were able to step right into the position. The worship team led by Craig and Valerie Tomlin were also able to provide anointed worship that kept the flow of God alive in the church. The rest of the staff have also stepped up and continue to go strong.

The church is doing great, growing in all areas under the leadership of the pastoral staff. This allows us to carry on with the vision the Lord appointed our congregation to take to international business and professional leaders. A number of other pastors and churches have been interested in what we have done. To them I would say: Prepare your church today as a city-focused or nation-focused church, so when the Lord calls for a change, you will be ready.

All of these changes, all of these paradigm shifts have a purpose. It is ultimately to fulfill the mandate of Scripture: "And He Himself gave some to be apostles, some prophets, some evangelists, and some pastors and teachers, for the equipping of the saints for the work of ministry..." (Ephes. 4:11-12).

There needs to be much more equipping done in the area of marketplace ministries, and God is going to hold the pastors, along with the evangelists, teachers, apostles, and prophets, responsible. We are not told to *do* the ministry; we are told to *equip others* to do the ministry. The word *equipping*, translated also as "perfecting" in the King James, or as "prepare" in the New International Version, basically means to put something into the condition that it should be in. It is used of nets being mended in Mark 1:19, and of sinners being restored in Galatians 6:1. When the net is mended, it is ready for its intended purpose of catching fish. When the one caught in a trespass is restored, he or she can continue in fellowship with the Lord and fulfill his or her purpose.

"Equipping" is to bring a person into the condition of being prepared to do whatever it is that God is calling for. As a pastor, a part of my equipping was in learning how to preach, how to study the Bible, how to deal with people, and the basics of counseling and so on. When we begin to equip kings for work in the marketplace, much of the training is the same as for any other Christian, but there are also some differences.

Businesspersons need to learn how to integrate their Christianity with the marketplace. The whole issue of the segregated life must be confronted. We need to eliminate the thinking that puts the secular and the sacred in two different categories that allows a person to sin at work while being "holy" at church. Your work and your ministry are not mutually exclusive, but rather fit very well under the one heading: Christian. Ethics, integrity, character, and moral principles all need to be integrated into the marketplace.

I am excited that there are so many equipping opportunities being offered right now to the business leader, but I must challenge the pastors again: Don't make your kings go outside the church. Train them, equip them, and release them into the marketplace, and you will see a move of God like you have never seen before.

Endnotes

1. Bill Hamon, Christian International Business Network, *Vision for Success Workbook* (Santa Rosa Beach, FL, 1999).

2. *Wagner Leadership Institute Provisional Catalog* (Colorado Springs, CO: Wagner Leadership Institute, 1999).

3. *Nehemiah Partners Brochure* (Minneapolis, MN: Nehemiah Partners, 1999).

Chapter Ten

Relationship Between the Church and Business Community

Megan Doyle

And He Himself gave some to be apostles, some prophets, some evangelists, and some pastors and teachers, for the equipping of the saints for the work of ministry, for the edifying of the Body of Christ (Ephesians 4:11-12).

The community of the Church and the Christian business community are two vitally important entities that God wishes to unite in the powerful work of His Kingdom during the times that are upon us.

Today, in many churches across America, the Church and the business community act as separate entities. Imagine for a moment the consequences of this disunity. A majority of the church members sitting in the pews are business and professional people. They spend most of their waking hours at work. Imagine the lost opportunities for ministry because the business world is not recognized as a place for ministry to occur. Why has the business world been overlooked? What are the issues that bring separation between the Church and the business community? What are the barriers that keep them apart?

Cultural Differences

One area that brings misunderstanding is in the contrast of cultures between the Church and business community. If you are a CEO, a business owner or leader, you are probably visionary, with strong administrative skills, and can set a strategic business plan in place and accomplish it in record time. You probably work under the pressure of deadlines and set high goals for yourself. You are able to accomplish a lot in a short period of time. Out of necessity you have learned how to work with pressure and developed the skills to reach high goals. This is mandatory in order to compete in today's corporate world. Another advantage, you have access to finances from income and loans to equip the business with the employees, technology, and whatever else it needs to run efficiently.

The Church, however, does not usually have the funding necessary to operate at the efficiency level of the corporate world. This is one of the most important contrasts between the two. Mega-churches are one exception. They look and act like the corporate world in many ways, and are also better financed than most other churches. However, the average church in America functions quite differently.

The average church will rarely run with highly strategic operations like our businesses, or with the efficiency of corporate America. We need to understand the cultural differences between the two, and adjust our thinking accordingly, if we are to interact with and come alongside ministries and churches.

In addition to the contrast in culture, most pastors are not CEOs. They are shepherds and preachers, a far different calling from corporate executive officer. Shepherds and preachers are concerned about things like member relationships, studying God's Word for the Sunday message, and directing their flock. The business matters of the church are often not a first priority, and resolving business matters is usually not part of the gifting of shepherd and pastor.

The limitations in funding specifically create a difficult environment for the pastor. He is expected to wear many hats and be an expert in several fields simultaneously. Some of those are: real estate, psychology, finance, preaching, teaching, and leading the flock. No one can be an expert in all of these areas, and most congregations cannot afford to hire the services or pay additional staff to provide these services.

We need to accept our churches' basic inefficiencies and the reasons for them. It is difficult to do. Our minds often do not work that way because we have been trained for a business world that excels in efficiency. We must be on guard to keep in check our potential frustration over encountering such a different culture. We must be careful to not withdraw over our frustrations with church inefficiency.

Withdrawal is the opposite of relationship. In fact, building relationships with your pastor is the first step toward addressing these issues. As businesspeople we can offer our skills and talents to the church in its areas of need. I know of one retired executive who has a permanent volunteer position in my local church, which has provided an office and support staff to assist him. His job is to coordinate all the volunteers in the church.

A friend of ours, Victor Eagan, has decreased his workweek by one day, and gives that day to the church. Another CEO we know, Steve Heinz, has sold his business and now holds a full-time volunteer position in his church. It is important that we seek the Lord to discern if He is leading us to help our church in the areas of our expertise. It does not need to be a full-time position, or even a part-time position. Seek the Lord on how you might become involved in your church, and remember to start that involvement by first building a relationship with your pastor.

Building Relationships

The importance of relationship is another area of cultural difference. In our business culture we are usually very short on true relationships. Relationships take time to develop, and business-people use their time setting priorities and getting things done. Deep, life-changing relationships are often not a priority in the business world, and that is where we need the help of the pastors. Relationship is the basis from which the Body of Christ springs forth—relationship with Christ first, and then with each other. Without relationships, visions die, projects fail, people are misunderstood, and divisions can set in. Without relationships the Kingdom of God cannot exist, and souls cannot be won to Christ.

Set Aside the Urgency

It is important that we put aside our sense of urgency and, instead, spend time building relationships and trust with our pastors and ministry leaders. Out of relationship will come the understanding and fellowship necessary to bridge the differences in our two cultures.

Checking Your Motives

In every relationship and every assignment from God, we must always check the motives of our heart. Why are we developing this relationship and why are we accepting this assignment? Are our egos involved? Are we looking for personal gain, power or control, or are we fully emptied of ourselves so that the Lord can freely use us?

The motives of some businesspeople have hurt their relationships with their pastors. A desire for power and control have often been found at the root of a businessperson's reasons for involvement. I have seen businesspeople try to control a church through board membership. Small rural churches are often the victims of such controlling boards. Sometimes the board will determine everything for the church—even what the pastor can preach about! No wonder pastors often tell me they are wary of businesspeople!

Businesspeople must be sensitive to the intimidating effect their worldly power and prosperity can have on pastors. Intimidation is not a very good foundation for building relationships. If our motives are pure, and we are sensitive to the differences between the church and business arena, relationships should not be hindered.

Power and control show up often, and seriously, in the area of church finance. Giving large amounts of money with the strings still attached is one way to control. The truth is, providing the funding for a project does not give someone the right to then dictate how the project should be accomplished. The opposite, refusal to give, can also be used as a passive method of control. All of our giving needs to be placed in the hands of God, led by the Spirit and not our flesh.

The Bible says in many places that our hearts are wicked and easily deceive us. Jeremiah 17:9-10 says, "The heart is deceitful above all things, and desperately wicked; who can know it? I, the Lord, search the heart, I test the mind, even to give every man according to his ways, according to the fruit of his doings."

King David was well acquainted with the impurities of his heart when the Spirit drew him to write these words in Psalm 139:23-24: "Search me, O God, and know my heart; try me, and know my anxieties; and see if there is any wicked way in me, and lead me in the way everlasting." We should pray this before the Lord, to protect us from impure motives in all the things we do.

Avoiding the Fund-raising Clash

Another finance-related area of division between the church and businesspeople occurs in the area of fund-raising. In this area it has often been pastors and ministry leaders who have hurt many businesspeople. Fund-raising for church and ministry definitely needs to occur with tact and sensitivity. The problem for businesspersons is when they are targeted for their money to the exclusion of anything else they have to offer—even to the exclusion of relationship. There are many businesspeople who believe their only purpose for the Kingdom of God is to provide funding. This leaves them frustrated and unfilled. The Christian businessperson can do much more than "offer provision for those with vision." In fact, giving financially is a part of every believer's life. Every Christian is called to give. Giving usually does not constitute an entire call, although there are those who possess the gift of giving.

One of the greatest schemes of satan is to polarize or even alienate businesspeople from pastors in this area, so that giving is either hindered or stopped. The result? The Church remains in a poverty mentality, believing that God will not bring in the necessary funds for the vision He gave them; and the businessperson misses an opportunity to be blessed for giving. Businesspeople need the blessings that come from giving, to fully walk in God's call on their lives. We are hindered when we do not give the Lord what He asks of us. It is an act of spiritual worship. When we give in this spirit, God can bless our giving.

Overlooked No Longer

Apart from finances, businesspeople are calling out to the Church to be fully recognized for their value and giftings for the Kingdom of God. The business community is a very important resource for this work. Some businesspeople hold powerful positions in society, and can use their influence on behalf of the Kingdom. If the Church began to reach out to, equip and release businesspeople, God's earthly Kingdom would look much different. What would happen if businesspeople began to pray for their emloyees? What if they began to understand that God has given them earthly authority for spiritual reasons? What if they realized they really have a pastor's heart for their employees?

Businesspeople have indeed been overlooked for the multitude of talents, skills, and gifts that could be utilized on behalf of God. It is a huge oversight. The spiritual and physical magnitude of what they have to offer is endless.

Businesspeople have not been trained and equipped for Kingdom work in the business arena. The Book of Ephesians tells us about the importance of this.

And He Himself gave some to be apostles, some prophets, some evangelists, and some pastors and teachers, for the equipping of the saints for the work of ministry, for the edifying of the Body of Christ (Ephesians 4:11-12).

Relationship Between the Church and Business Community

God calls businesspeople just as He calls pastors and ministry leaders. Sometimes the call on a businessperson's life is misunderstood as a drive toward materialism, or their motivation is mistaken as greed. Businesspeople are all called to create commerce, jobs and wealth, and to add to the economy. God strategically places them in their career positions for His intended purposes. They don't arrive in their positions through a good resumé, a good education, or a lucky break. They arrive through the divine providence of God.

If church leaders and businesspeople can overcome the obstacles we have spoken of, and can come together with pure hearts, led by the Holy Spirit, an important bridge between the Church and the business community will be built. The result will be amazing. Frozen funds will be released and businesspeople will be empowered in a new way to become all God has created them to be. This will bring spiritual change to the workplace, as unbelievers sit up and take notice that their leaders are beginning to look at their businesses through spiritual eyes. God's Kingdom will advance as never before, and God will be glorified!

Chapter Eleven

Testimony of Dennis and Megan Doyle

Megan Doyle

Freely you have received, freely give (Matthew 10:8b).

My husband, Dennis, and I reside in Minneapolis, Minnesota with our two children Devin and Nathan. We own a full-service, commercial real estate company with offices in seven cities and over 400 employees.

A few years ago the Lord began to show us He not only had a specific call on our lives individually, but also had a call on our company. At first we were surprised by the idea that God might be interested in our business. When we began to pray about it, and hold this idea up to the light of Scripture, we saw that God indeed uses not only individuals, but also cities, people groups, and even nations to accomplish His will. Why then, couldn't He use a business?

The idea did not come easily to us; it was a process. As we prayed for our business, we began to look at it in terms of its purpose. This began at a time when we were struggling with some major issues concerning our company. One of the options we were considering at the time was selling the business so that Dennis could help other ministries full time. In the midst of this decision-making, we were hosting an event for Ed Silvoso's ministry, Harvest Evangelism. Dennis and I both sit on the international board of this ministry. We have supported Ed, and have grown spiritually through our relationship with him, as well as through his remarkable teaching.

During the event we were hosting for Ed, another board member, Rich Marshall, mentioned to us that he felt God impressing a message for us upon his spirit. Dennis felt the message would be a confirmation to sell the business. I disagreed. I felt God was going to have us approach our business in a new way. The next morning, we met with Rich and his wife, Wilma, and Rich shared his heart with us. He said he felt the Lord wanted us to keep the business, and begin to look at it through spiritual eyes. He told Dennis to stop trying to leave his business to help other ministries and, instead, focus that energy on his company. Continuing, Rich suggested we begin to view our employees with the heart of a pastor. This kind of thinking was revolutionary for Dennis and me. In the past, we had viewed the business as being separate from the Kingdom of God. We saw it more as a means to an end—a way to provide a living and build a retirement so we could then serve the Lord freely. If anything, we saw the business as an interference to serving God, not as a means to serve Him.

As we carefully compared Rich's advice with Scripture, we both felt God confirm in our hearts the validity of what Rich had perceived. God showed us a whole new model that day, and it would have a major impact on the rest of our lives. We realized that part of God's call on our lives included both how we handled our spiritual responsibility for our employees and how well we practiced His stewardship principles in the business.

Discovering Our Company's Purpose

Our overall thinking changed quickly with this new revelation. We began to see the business in a new way. We realized that it had a spiritual purpose as well as a financial purpose. We began to seek God about what the specific spiritual or redemptive purpose of our business might be. As a result we feel we have uncovered a threefold purpose for the business, which includes prayer, giving, and our testimony.

A Prayer Strategy

The first purpose involves the use of prayer in a powerful way. Through the ministry of Ed Silvoso and his leadership in the prayer evangelism movement, both in Argentina and the United States, we have become familiar with the concepts of prayer evangelism. "If prayer evangelism worked in neighborhoods, sports teams and schools," we asked ourselves, "why wouldn't it work in a business?" With the teachings in Ed Silvoso's book, *That None Should Perish*,[1] as our foundation, we developed a strategy of prayer for our business.

Prayer evangelism is a biblical concept, which entails praying for everyone in a particular neighborhood, school, or business, as First Timothy instructs:

> *Therefore I exhort first of all that supplications, prayers, intercessions, and giving of thanks be made for all men, for kings and all who are in authority, that we may lead a quiet and peaceable life in all godliness and reverence. For this is good and acceptable in the sight of God our Savior, who desires all men to be saved and to come to the knowledge of the truth* (1 Timothy 2:1-4).

Taking this advice, we pray for each individual employee of our business at least once a month. For those in authority, we pray more often, lifting up the senior executives to the Lord on a weekly and sometimes daily basis.

We bless each person and his family, asking God, through His love, to shower His grace and goodness in each of their lives. We also ask God's love to protect them and prosper them. We pray for every property we manage, and the person or institution who owns them.

The power of prayer seems to have a calming effect on the business and the employees, and has also changed the attitude of our hearts toward them. It has given us a deeper burden for their welfare, which causes us to pray even more. Another benefit, some of our employees have started Bible studies or prayer meetings at the office. We encourage this, and have seen the faith of those involved grow. We keep our involvement with the Bible studies or prayer groups minimal, so as not to intimidate the employees who do not attend.

Every Tuesday morning at 7:00 a.m., eight to ten prayer partners join us in our home to pray for the business. At these meetings, we seek God for His overall direction for the company, as well as giving thanks and praise to Him. We also offer petitions and requests on behalf of the business, the employees, and our prayer partners. We believe God answers prayer. It is the only power in the universe that can move the hand of God.

Also, the enemy cannot stand in the presence of a blessing. He cannot tolerate the glory of God; so through the power of blessing, those blessed are protected from the enemy. In this way, when the gospel is presented through our witness, people are not encumbered by the enemy.

We also pray for our competition. First Timothy 2:1 exhorts us to pray for all people. So we ask God to bless our competition in every city where we have an office. We believe competition, with integrity, is good for the economy and good for our business, challenging us to always be the very best we can be in every business situation.

Giving of Ourselves

The second part of the redemptive purpose of the business involves giving of time, talents, and financial resources. One way we do this is by helping charities and/or ministries with their real estate needs. The extraordinary need in this area has led us to develop a division that works primarily with non-profit organizations. We offer complimentary help through the business as well as offering our services through our non-profit division. We also provide our employees with opportunities to give to inner-city ministries through food and clothing drives. We try to encourage them to volunteer their time, talent, and skills to those in need. The employees feel good about an opportunity to be involved and are blessed for their actions.

In addition, we have formed a personal foundation that is funded by a percentage of pre-tax profits from the business. The purpose of the foundation is to finance Christian causes. In this way the business is not only blessed through the giving of time and talents, but is also blessed through giving financially. Dennis and I also give our time and talent to these causes, and believe in tithing personally. We are very grateful to be able to serve the Lord through giving. There is no greater blessing personally than to give from what has been given to us.

We believe in the complete sovereignty of Jesus Christ and have experienced His great love for us. We trust Him not only with our business, but also with our very lives.

> *He is the image of the invisible God, the firstborn over all creation. For by Him all things were created that are in heaven and that are on earth, visible and invisible, whether thrones or dominions or principalities or powers. All things were created through Him and for Him* (Colossians 1:15-16).

These verses beautifully testify to the sovereignty of Christ. As a result we have dedicated not only our lives as a living sacrifice to the Lord, but we have also dedicated the business to the Lord, freely giving back what He has given us.

A Testimony to Other Businesses

The third purpose we discovered is to be a beacon of light to other businesses and businesspeople. We offer our testimony as a model of how God has led us to minister right where we are, how we see business as a ministry. We also speak at many conferences worldwide, explaining spiritual principles for the business world. We pray for, encourage, and counsel other Christian businesspeople who would like to apply Christian principles to their businesses.

The result? We have enjoyed wonderful success. Our real estate business has tripled since we started praying; however, success does not come without a price. God often uses the thing most important to us to test our faith and develop our character. We have had bitter losses as well as great accomplishments. Through it all, our lives have become more sanctified, and each day we are slowly being made into the image of Christ. We are praying over our employees' lives, and the business continues to prosper.

We have seen God answer prayer situations too numerous to list. We are deeply grateful for Ed Silvoso and the godly impact he has had on our lives. Through Ed, God dramatically changed our lives for better, and has drawn us into a deeper and more meaningful relationship with Him.

We know firsthand the powerful effect of Rich Marshall's revelation as written in this book. This message will touch businesspeople deep within their hearts. It will speak to your lives in a transforming way. It will free you to be the person God has called you to be, without doubt or guilt. For many, it will bring a new peace in your spirit through the assurance that you can work in the world of business, and still be in God's will. We praise God for His life-giving message through Rich and this book, and we are thankful for Rich's obedience in proclaiming it.

Endnote

1. Silvoso, Ed, *That None Should Perish* (Ventura, CA: Regal Books, 1994).

Chapter Twelve

Releasing the Kings

Doing the will of God from the heart, with goodwill doing service, as to the Lord, and not to men (Ephesians 6:6b-7).

One man! One man faithful to God. Jeremiah Lanphier asked the Lord a simple question, "What wilt Thou have me to do?" and as a result, one million souls were saved in the United States alone. Plus, another million backsliders were called back to Christ.

Jeremiah Lanphier was called of God to spark the last great business revival.[1] It started in 1857 and continued for 40 years. Lanphier was asked by his church, the Old Dutch North Church, located at the corner of Fulton and William Streets in Manhattan, to become a "city missionary." That phrase in itself gives us great insight into this church. First of all, members wanted to reach the city. They were not content only with growing the local church. Secondly, we notice the missionary they chose was not a pastor, but a businessman. Here was a church that believed in the ministry of the "kings," and would assign the task of reaching the masses of New York City to a businessman. At that time the city had a population of 800,000, and our nation a population of 30 million.

A Simple Beginning

Jeremiah Lanphier began by visiting homes and introducing himself and his church. He focused first on immigrant families, but apparently he was having little success. The day came when he went into the back room of the church and prayed this prayer: "Lord, what wilt Thou have me to do?" It was then that the Lord led him to start a noontime prayer meeting. He went out into the crowded streets of the city and began to invite the thousands of businesspeople walking the crowded New York streets to join him for prayer. His church was located just a few blocks from Wall Street and just a few blocks from the current site of the World Trade Center.

Lanphier had a big booming voice that he used on the street corner to call the folks to prayer. He printed a handbill that invited them to an upstairs room in the church for prayer. Here is what it said:

> "How often shall I pray? As often as the language of prayer is in my heart. As often as I see my need of help. As often as I feel the power of temptation. As often as I am made sensible of any spiritual declension or feel the aggression of a worldly earthly spirit....
>
> "A day prayer meeting is held every Wednesday from 12-1 o'clock.... This meeting is intended to give merchants, clerks, strangers, and business men generally an opportunity to stop and call upon God amid the perplexities incident to their respective avocations. It will continue for one hour; but it is designed for those who may find it inconvenient to remain more than nine or ten minutes, as well as for those who can spare the whole hour. The necessary interruption will be slight because anticipated; and those who are in haste can often expedite their business engagements by halting to lift up their voices to the throne of grace in humble, grateful prayer."[2]

An Explosion

On September 23, 1857, Lanphier started his first prayer meeting, and no one showed up. He prayed alone for 35 minutes, and then heard footsteps on the staircase as four more people joined him. The next week there were 14, and the week following that, 23. They decided to meet daily, and the group soon grew to 100. Before long there were a thousand meeting daily, so they added meetings at 6:00 a.m. and 9:00 a.m., continuing to meet at noon, as before.

As the prayer movement exploded, over 20 meetings were held in New York City. By the spring of 1858, theaters that seated 2,500 people were full 30 minutes before starting time. Over 6,000 gathered at the noon hour in New York City. But the revival was not to be confined to that city alone. It soon spread to Philadelphia; Pittsburgh; Washington DC; Chicago; Kalamazoo; Michigan; and Mobile, Alabama; to name just a few. In Boston a gentleman rose to say that he had just come from Omaha, Nebraska and had been able to attend a prayer meeting in various cities all across America. The revival soon spread to San Francisco on the West Coast as well.

Carried By the Wind

There was no e-mail and no one carried a cell phone, but the word of this prayer revival in the marketplace spread rapidly across the nation. It would also find its way into Canada, England, Scotland, and Wales. The people met in churches, and also in theaters, college campuses, and even saloons. The revival swept onto the campus of Harvard University in 1858. Five thousand people gathered for prayer in the Academy of Music Hall in Washington, DC. In Chicago, 2,000 gathered for prayer in the Metropolitan Theater every day. Churches were packed for prayer at 7:00 a.m., noon, and 6:30 p.m. daily. Even the riverboats on the Mississippi River had people gathering for prayer.

In Kalamazoo, Michigan, at the very first prayer meeting, before anyone even prayed, the businessman leader read a prayer request. It was from a wife asking for prayer for her husband: "Please pray for my husband's conversion. He is far from God and needs our prayers." A lawyer then stood up and announced that his wife must have written the note, that he fit the description, and she was praying for him. Before he could make his way to the front, a blacksmith arose and said it must have been his wife. Before they could begin the meeting, five men were saved, and before long, 500 in that city were converted to Christ!

This revival was not confined to the church. In some cities even the fire and police departments opened their doors for prayer. This revival was approaching that which the Lord promised when He said, "I will pour out of My Spirit on all flesh" (Acts 2:17). Even the local newspapers picked up the story and carried reports of the revival. Following is an excerpt from an article in the *Chicago Daily Press* of March 13, 1858:

> "A large class of our readers, we are assured, will be interested in such details as we have been able to collect in a form meeting our purpose, to the extent to which Chicago has shared in the general religious awakening that has been one of the most marked events of the year throughout the entire country, East and West.
>
> "In the larger cities of the East and in New York City especially, this movement, in the increased zeal of Christians and the awakening and conversion of those previously unconcerned and careless in religious matters, has become a prominent topic among the news of the day, so large a portion of those communities have been sharing in and yielding to the influences at work which has had steady, silent and solemn progress, without noise or excitement."[3]

This was a revival that shook all corners of society for God. It was a revival that resulted in church growth, evangelism, and a change in the communities. The phrase, "changing the spiritual climate of the city" has recently come into use to describe the potential of a large number of open hearts, where God moves more rapidly and easily than in the past. That phrase could have well described America in 1858 and 1859. In one crowded prayer meeting a man was praying when his neighbor gave him a shove with his elbow, grabbed his arm, and said, "Stop praying and tell me how I can become a Christian." Reports from that era tell us that the presence of God was so strong that when ships would glide into New York Harbor, the people aboard would begin repenting. Charles Finney said that people seemed to prefer meetings for prayer to those for preaching. He wrote that "the windows of Heaven were opened and the Spirit of God poured out like a flood."[4] That is the kind of spiritual climate and atmosphere that I am expecting again very soon.

This revival would also affect the nations of the world. I have mentioned Canada, England, Scotland, and Wales, but it would also move into Africa and Asia as well. When word of the revival in the United States spread to Cape Town, South Africa, local Christians convened a conference. They were surprised when 374 Christian leaders showed up. They began to pray for an outpouring of God's Spirit in Africa. Fifty days later at a youth camp a young black girl recounted: "There was a sound like an approaching tornado. All the youth at once rose to their feet and began to pray. When the minister in charge of the camp asked his youth director for an explanation of this strange behavior of the youth, the answer was, 'It's the presence of God.' The minister replied, 'I hold you responsible.' Nevertheless, prayer meetings multiplied in Africa."[5]

More Than Fear

What was the spiritual atmosphere in America when the revival broke out? Civil war was looming and a major stock market crash was on the horizon. The revival started in September and was in full bloom by late October. It was about that time that Wall Street suffered a major crash. One revival historian says that you cannot call the move of God in 1857–1859 a revival because of the stock market crash. He explains that this was not a revival, but just people reaching out to God in response to the terrible financial times our nation was experiencing.

However, God in His sovereignty had set the revival in motion before the stock market crash. And even if He hadn't, what is wrong with people reaching out to God in times of trouble and need?

My study shows that the revival occurred in both the North and South. This revival began to wane about the same time that the Civil War started, but on the front lines of that conflict, thousands were converted to Christ. One report states that 150,000 men were converted during the war.

Jeremiah Lanphier had no idea of the impact of his one-sentence prayer to God in the back room of his church that day in September 1857. Preachers such as Charles Spurgeon, Charles Finney, Dwight L. Moody, and missionaries like Hudson Taylor were all impacted by this revival. Their names have been written in history as mighty men of God, and that they were. But up next to these priests' names, we must inscribe the name of one of God's kings: Jeremiah Lanphier.

Calling Another Wind

I have the conviction that what God has done in the past He will do again. And I believe that where He has poured out His Spirit in the past, He will pour it out again. With that in mind, Dr. Paul Cox and I went to New York City one cold December morning and stood on the corner of Fulton and William Streets. We asked the Lord to meet us there, and to give us what He had given to Jeremiah Lanphier. Paul Cox is an American Baptist pastor with tremendous spiritual discernment. While I might stand there and discern nothing, Paul is able to sense the presence of the Lord, or even any other spirit that might be there. As the cold wind blew, he began to feel the warmth of the Lord's presence. We stayed until we were assured that we had received what we came for. We now call it simply, "The Jeremiah Lanphier anointing." It is an anointing for revival in the marketplace, and you can have it as well. Paul and I have passed it on every opportunity that we have had. It is operating in over 30 cities in the United States, Singapore, Mexico, Guatemala, Argentina, Canada, and South Africa.

For 11 chapters you have been reading about a mighty move of God in the marketplace, and now we have just observed one from over 140 years ago. I believe we will soon see this kind of power in our own day. I can see it now with the eyes of faith, and you can too. It's coming. God has promised it! We don't know when, but we are getting ready. I have been studying revivals for years now. In the beginning, I loved to read of these great moves of God in the past. But I will tell you, I don't want to keep on studying and researching and reading about revivals of the past. I want to see one. I want to be a part of it—to taste it, feel it, smell it—I want it all.

Oh, and I have seen some. I've witnessed the move of God in Argentina, Guatemala, Korea, Toronto, and various American cities. As I mentioned, the revival in Argentina has been going strong since 1982. I have been traveling to Argentina to see this revival firsthand since 1987. I currently go there twice a year with Harvest Evangelism where we present the Argentine revival as a model to the hundreds from around the world who attend the Harvest conferences. Through the leadership of Ed Silvoso and his top vice president, David Thompson, we are able to join the Harvest team in Argentina and key apostolic pastors and leaders in that nation, to assist them in taking the revival to cities of Argentina as well. A number of Argentine cities have been impacted through the strategic city-reaching plans of Harvest Evangelism. Ed is a native Argentine, and Dave and Sue Thompson served for a number of years in Argentina and have the respect of the church leaders there as well as around the world.

C. Peter Wagner has done considerable research in Argentina and writes about it in his book, *Revival! It Can Transform Your City.*[6] He selects three top means of sustaining revival from a much longer possible list of key components. From his three, I will focus on only one for our purposes in this book.

The top three means of sustaining the Argentine revival according to Wagner are: (1) Focus from day one on winning the lost. "Jesus did not come to earth *primarily* to solve social problems or to get more people praying or to make peace among religious factions of the day. He came primarily to die on the cross and rise again so that people could have their sins forgiven and be saved";

(2) Taking authority over all the forces of the enemy; (3) Having the apostolic order in place.[7]

Let's consider the "apostolic order." Until recent years, the teaching from Ephesians chapter 4 regarding the fivefold ministry gifts of apostle, prophet, evangelist, pastor, and teacher were considered relevant by only a small minority of Christians. As the modern Pentecostal and Charismatic movements have enlarged and become such a powerful force in world missions and church growth, we are hearing more about the two forgotten gifts: apostle and prophet. Even in more conservative and evangelical circles there is increasing teaching about the apostle and prophet. For a better understanding of the subject, I recommend these two books: *Apostles and the Emerging Apostolic Movement* by David Cannistraci[8] and *Churchquake* by C. Peter Wagner.[9]

Wagner refers to the leaders of the Argentine revival as the apostles of that revival. They are friends with each other, pray for each other, and cheer each other on. He points out that there are "apostles of the city" as well as "apostles in the churches." The "apostle in the city" is a concept that we need to develop. While the Argentines have learned about this, we seem to have missed it here in America. We need to operate under the guidelines outlined in Ephesians chapter 4, not only in the Church, but also in the broader context of entire cities. It is important that we begin to see and identify the citywide leaders who can lead the entire Church within a city in strategic plans to reach that city. Wagner says, "This deficiency needs urgent attention."

In the coming revival we need to identify the apostolic leaders in the marketplace arena. God is going to begin to reveal the fivefold ministry gifts to them as they operate in the marketplace. I believe we will soon see prophets and apostles in business, government, and all facets of society. As these apostolic kings begin to operate, we will have the opportunity to see the revival I have been describing. Revival always requires a person who God uses to both spark and lead it. We can identify these people in the Bible, in history, and in today's revivals. With that in mind, we will also be able to identify the leader or leaders of the coming marketplace revival.

Who are they? They are kings. They are called. They walk in a power and authority that can break the grip of bondage and oppression holding many. They are a new breed of ministers that God is raising up for this day.

Endnotes

1. Elana Lynse, *Flames of Revival* (Westchester, IL: Crossway Books, a division of Good News Publishers, 1989).

There are numerous books written about the revival that Jeremiah Lanphier led. For the purposes of this book, I am using, and recommend, only one of those books: *Flames of Revival* by Elana Lynse. For a number of years this prayer warrior was a member of our church in Sunnyvale, and now resides in the Tampa, Florida area. I am indebted for her excellent research on Jeremiah Lanphier.

2. ibid., reference to a secondary source, 62.

3. ibid., reference to a secondary source, 66.

4. ibid., reference to a secondary source, 68.

5. ibid., reference to a secondary source, 68-69.

6. C. Peter Wagner, *Revival, It Can Transform Your City* (Colorado Springs, CO: Wagner Institute for Practical Ministry, 1999).

7. Ibid., 41-47.

8. David Cannistraci, *Apostles and the Emerging Apostolic Movement* (Ventura, CA: Regal Books, 1996).

9. C. Peter Wagner, *Churchquake* (Ventura, CA: Regal Books, 1999).

Chapter Thirteen

Transforming the Marketplace

Then He said to them, "The harvest truly is great, but the laborers are few; therefore pray the Lord of the harvest to send out laborers into His harvest" (Luke 10:2).

Wilma and I were attending a strategic business consultation sponsored by The Nehemiah Partners when Cindy Jacobs informed me she had a word from the Lord for me. She said the Lord had given her this word the night before, and at the close of the evening service, she would speak it to me. I had already received other prophetic revelations from Cindy that had proved to be very accurate, and so I was happily anticipating what she had to say. I was also glad to know in advance that the word was coming, because in the past when she had spoken over me, I would become so overwhelmed by the power of the Spirit that I would miss the last part of the word. This time I was determined to stay focused and hear it in its entirety.

When Cindy called me to the front, I firmly planted my feet and prepared myself to hear the entire word. She began, "Rich, the Lord says He wants to give to you the mantle of Jeremiah Lanphier." With that one sentence, the Spirit of the Lord took over and I did not hear the rest of what Cindy had to say. I was immediately directed by the Lord with regard to what I was to do. Cindy did not know that I had studied the life of Lanphier, and with just the mention of his name, the Lord began to speak to me about the prayer meetings He would use to spark a new city-transforming move of the Spirit. Before she was finished speaking, I had the direction from the Lord that has taken Wilma and me to dozens of cities and several nations.

The movement that Lanphier led is called the "Prayer Revival" or the "Business Man's Revival" in historical records. I like both of these descriptions because I believe prayer will spark the coming marketplace transformation more than anything else; and I believe the Lord will use a businessperson to lead it. The Lord gave very clear direction regarding my involvement in this coming move of God. He has sent me forth with a message of release for the business and professional leaders to see ministry and business as one and the same thing, and He has given me an equipping mandate with regard to prayer in the marketplace.

Based on the model of Jeremiah Lanphier, the Lord led me to organize "Marketplace Lighthouses of Prayer." Lanphier's prayer meetings that started at noon soon met at all hours of the day, and this is the case with prayer meetings that God is raising up in our generation as well. They may start at 6:00 a.m. or as late as 5:30 p.m. The ingredient that ties them together is not the time, but the fact that they are all led by "kings" and follow an agenda outlined by the Lord in Luke chapter 10.

When the Lord spoke the message about Jeremiah Lanphier to me through the prophetic word spoken by Cindy Jacobs, He had already begun to redirect our steps. After pastoring local churches for over 35 years, we knew that things were changing with regard to our ministry, but we did not know the form the new direction would take. When Cindy said, "The Lord says to place on you the mantle of Jeremiah Lanphier," immediately everything changed.

Less than one month later, Wilma and I laid our hands on our copastors Scott and Janet Abke and installed them as pastors of the church that the Lord had led us to start years before. The leaders of the church then commissioned Wilma and me as apostolic leaders for the marketplace. We remain on staff at the church, with a traveling ministry to kings around the world.

The Lord has directed us to challenge business leaders with the story of Lanphier and ask them to conduct marketplace prayer meetings in 30 specific cities in America. Today, those prayer meetings are forming a catalytic force from the West Coast to the East, and in major Midwest cities as well. Business leaders in Monterrey, Mexico; Pretoria, South Africa; and in various Central and South American cities have heard the story of Lanphier and are asking God to use them as He did this man over 140 years ago.

It is time to recognize that the "call of God" can be into a priestly ministry role, or into a kingly ministry role. We must establish the fact that a person need not leave their current profession to "go into the ministry," but recognize that their profession *is* "their ministry." Now we can create an atmosphere in the marketplace for business leaders to unite for global spiritual impact. And we can release the potential of these leaders through the power of prayer, to bring healing to the hurting, prosperity to the needy, and the full operation of Kingdom principles in the marketplace.

The Lord directed me to use Luke chapter 10, where Jesus sends out the 70, as a model for the Marketplace Lighthouses of Prayer. Ed Silvoso uses this Scripture often when teaching city-reaching methods. It works equally well as an outline for a prayer meeting. If you want to begin one of these prayer meetings I encourage you to use this model:

> *After these things the Lord appointed seventy others also, and sent them two by two before His face into every city and place where He Himself was about to go. Then He said to them, "The harvest truly* **is** *great, but the laborers* **are** *few; therefore pray the Lord of the harvest to send out laborers into His harvest. Go your way; behold, I send you out as lambs among wolves. Carry neither money bag, knapsack, nor sandals; and greet no one along the road. But whatever house you enter, first say, 'Peace*

to this house.' And if a son of peace is there, your peace will rest on it; if not, it will return to you. And remain in the same house, eating and drinking such things as they give, for the laborer is worthy of his wages. Do not go from house to house. Whatever city you enter, and they receive you, eat such things as are set before you. And heal the sick there, and say to them, 'The kingdom of God has come near to you' " (Luke 10:1-9).

Here the Lord sends out the nameless and faceless leaders. They are sent as lambs among wolves, and I'm sure that many of you who are going into the marketplace may feel very much like they did. Notice the four directives they received from the Lord. I use them as an outline for prayer meetings.

1. "First say, 'Peace to this house.' " We start with a time of blessing.

The prayer time should begin with a time of blessing each person present. The blessing can include a blessing on their family, business, and their dreams. These prayers of blessing should be offered out loud, and when possible, all participants will focus attention on the one being blessed. It is important that this time of prayer be conducted in a very "non-religious" way. When you bow your head and close your eyes, you immediately close out the ones who may need the prayer the most. If someone walks by the room and looks in, it should be an inviting and welcome atmosphere. If you have a group of four or five, then each of you can bless the others. If the group is larger, divide into groups of four or five and spend the opening moments of the prayer meeting by blessing.

The word *bless* basically means, "to speak good words," and words of blessing are words like *joy, peace, happiness, fulfillment,* and *destiny*. As you speak these words, look the person in the face and smile. That will make it very inviting to others who also need to receive the blessing of the Lord.

Jesus told the disciples to speak peace to the wolves to whom they were being sent. Therefore, I am sure we can speak peace and blessing to all.

2. "Eating and drinking such things as they give." Spend time in casual conversation and eating and drinking together.

We have all been to prayer meetings where it was all business and we never even got acquainted with the ones we were praying with. Those who come to the marketplace prayer meetings must feel the love and compassion of those they are praying with, and they need an opportunity to hear the heartfelt concerns of each one. This means that we establish a relaxed and comfortable atmosphere.

3. "And heal the sick there." At this point we pray for the "felt needs" of those who are present.

Jesus sent out the 70 with the instructions to heal the sick, or to meet whatever the felt need of the person might be. We have found that in the marketplace setting, the needs are often business-related. As we pray for illnesses, business deals, marriages, relationships, and other needs, we expect God to bring a miracle. As the prayers are answered, the word will spread and others will want to be a part of this powerful meeting. Keep in mind, that up to this point in time, there has been no preaching of any kind. The pattern that Jesus gave was to bless, fellowship, pray for the felt needs, and then to:

4. "Say to them, 'The kingdom of God has come near to you.' "

This is time for faith and boldness. The only hope for our nation is the intervention of the living God. Pray for the President, pray for the leaders in your city, and yes, pray for the business leaders who shape the thinking and direction of our cities and nation. Ask God to impact the school campuses, homes, and businesses in your area.

Let me quickly run through the agenda again. First, we bless each person present, and we follow that with a casual time of fellowship. Refreshments or coffee, maybe pizza or a light meal can

131

fit right here. Then move to a time of praying for the felt needs of those present. The Lord has been moving in powerful ways in response to the prayers offered at the business prayer meetings. After those three points are concluded, you can declare, "The kingdom of God has come near to you."

Since these are prayer meetings, keep the focus on prayer. If there is to be any kind of proclamation at all, keep it short and at the end, after the prayers have been freely offered.

We have started literally hundreds of these prayer meetings in the marketplace, and we are believing God for thousands more. They work best when led by a king who has the support of a priest. This is one area in which the kings and priests can work together. In the Seattle area, Steve Gandara, a business leader, has started a number of these prayer meetings. He is strongly supported by his pastor, Sam Benson, but in the prayer meetings, Sam takes an out-of-the-limelight position, and Steve is the leader.

Steve sends out a weekly e-mail message with encouraging testimonies to all who attend, challenging men and women to bring their friends to the next meeting. In one of those messages he added this at the bottom: "Our Goal: Win the Northwest to the gospel by covering the airwaves with marketplace prayer meetings around the clock."

I was at the first meeting in the Seattle area, and during the time to pray for the felt needs, four or five requests were given. One was from a woman who said she had opened her mail just before coming to the 6:00 a.m. prayer meeting. She had been recently audited by the IRS and had thought she was completely free; however, in the mail was a $40,000 tax bill. She was devastated by this news. Steve called the group to pray for her. The next request came from a district manager for a major chain of stores. He felt that three store managers were going over his head in an effort to get him fired. In that case, we had him bless each of these managers. I was very impressed that he knew all the names of their wives and children and could bless each of them as well. Another request came from a man who wanted us to pray that he would double his business in 60 days.

By the next week, the praise reports were coming in. The IRS fully dismissed all costs including penalties and interest by the following Friday. The man whose managers had been endeavoring to get him fired reported that before the week was out, these same managers had called him and invited him to lunch. One of them said something like, "I am concerned about our relationship and I wanted to make sure things were right between us." The man who wanted to double his business in 60 days actually had his business double before lunch on Monday, the same day as the prayer meeting.

With these kinds of miracles in the marketplace, this move of God I am talking about cannot be far behind. Every week reports of answered prayers are heard from Seattle and many other cities as well. It is time for a marketplace revival, and I believe it is coming soon.

The next Jeremiah Lanphier could be a man or a woman. He could be an American or she might be an Argentine. This apostolic "king" could be a high-tech genius, or a blue-collar laborer. God is looking for someone whom He can anoint, someone who is willing to pray a prayer like Lanphier's: "Lord, what will You have me do for You?"

Conclusion

I...beseech you to walk worthy of the calling with which you were called (Ephesians 4:1).

Leaders come in all shapes and sizes, and attain their positions in any number of ways. Some are selected by popular choice; some gain their position through deceit and treachery. Some work hard at becoming a leader, while for others it is very easy and natural. Some gain leadership through wealth; others gain wealth through leadership.

Kings also come in all shapes and sizes. However, they are all selected in the same way. God chooses them! He selects—anoints—appoints. They may have different attitudes about their roles. Some of the kings may be fearful and reluctant, with a sense of unworthiness and almost overwhelmed by the task. Others enter into the kingly anointing with a faith and confidence that they can conquer all.

The common ingredient is this: They know that God has called them, and that God will enable them. They know the power is from the Lord, and they know they can walk humbly before the Lord with a boldness that defies human reasoning.

Are you one of those kings? If you are, it is time for your coronation! This is the day!

Take some time right now to respond to the call of God. Join me in this commitment:

Father God, I humbly come before You as the King of kings. I submit myself under the mighty hand of God, and ask You to do the work in my life that You desire to do. I willingly give over the control of my life to You, and determine to walk in Your ways. I know that You desire to move mightily in the earth, and I offer myself to be used by You. I know that there is a kingly anointing for business, and I ask You to grant it to me. I promise to faithfully use the weapons You give me, and to exert the authority that comes to me for Your Kingdom. I recognize that my role as king is as a servant to You, the King. Use me to bring about a city- and nation-transforming move of God that helps to usher in the endtime harvest. In the name of Jesus, the King of kings, I pray. Amen.

What has been written here came out of "prophetic revelation." God has used many people to spark it, and He has called me into many hours of study to discern it. But under the surface, apart from all that, there is a prophetic revelation, a word from the living God, an insight that did not come from man. It is powerful because it comes from God. I believe it to be an important piece in the city-transformation puzzle; it might just be *the* missing piece, that when put in place, makes the whole complete. I know it is a freeing word. Business and professional people will find a new release and anointing. It is a freeing word for pastors as well. Those whose hearts are open to receive will be greatly blessed.

In the pages of this book we have seen the "army that God is raising up for the coming harvest." This is an army that is made up of the entire Body of Christ, and at the core is an army staffed by business and professional people. I know God is calling to His kings today. Listen for that call, and respond!

Epilogue

After working in the church system for many years, my wife, Wilma, and I have been a bit surprised by the truth we are discovering about God's anointing for business in this high tech society. However, a few years ago the Lord nudged us to look in new places and to consider new leaders for the transforming work of the Lord.

The day the Lord connected us with Dennis and Megan Doyle is probably the day that the seeds for this book were sown. We had been serving for a number of years on the board of Harvest Evangelism, a city-reaching ministry founded and led by Ed Silvoso. Dennis and Megan had just recently joined the board but were already actively involved in many aspects of leadership. In fact, the meeting we were attending that summer was one that they were hosting.

During a time of worship and fellowship with each other and the Lord, I began to sense the Lord giving me a word of encouragement for Dennis. These impressions were so strong that I knew I needed to tell him.

I said, "Dennis, I believe the Lord has a word for you."

"I'd like to hear it," he responded.

He seemed tremendously eager to hear it, so I asked if Wilma and I could have some private time with him and Megan in the morning. That gave me a chance to pray and seek the Lord and make sure that I was hearing right, and to make sure I was ready to speak these words by God's Spirit.

I have learned to be very careful with giving out these "words," and I speak a caution here about claiming divine revelation for every thought that enters one's mind. I know that God can and does speak to His children. When He does, it is wonderful. But I have seen the other side as well. I have seen the flesh in operation and have felt the pain of persons who were "prophesied" over, and then were terribly disappointed and disillusioned when the "word" did not come to pass. Does God speak today? Absolutely! Do we hear Him right all the time? No!

Dr. Jack Deere writes: "Today, after years of practical experience and intense study on the subject of God's speaking, I am convinced that God does indeed speak apart from the Bible, though never in contradiction to it. And he speaks to all his children, not just to specially gifted prophetic people. And he will speak to us all in amazing detail."[1]

In John 10:3b (NKJV) we read: "The sheep hear His voice; and He calls His own sheep by name and leads them out." What a thought! God calls His sheep—us—by name. And we know the voice of the Shepherd! Max Lucado, in his book *When God Whispers Your Name*, reminds us that God has even written your name on His hand.[2] How does that sound? Your name on God's hand, and your name spoken by God's voice!

Both Jack Deere[3] and Cindy Jacobs[4] have excellent books on hearing the voice of God. While this has not been a book about hearing the voice of God, I have heard that voice often and have referred to it many times. So let me give a little perspective on the topic: When I use the term *hear*, I am not referring to hearing the audible voice of God, but rather to that which I hear in my heart or in my mind. I know of some people who have heard the audible voice of God, and that is fully consistent with Scripture. God also speaks in dreams and visions, and in numerous other ways (see Num. 12:1-8). What I am referring to might be called an "impression" or an "insight." I know it is the Lord because of the

138

context of the message. For instance, there are certain things that satan will not say to us. He is not an encourager, but rather a deceiver. When I am receiving "words" about my destiny, about God's plan and purposes for my life, I can know that those words are from the Lord. The "words" that come from God are meant for edification, exhortation and comfort (see 1 Cor. 14:3). When I enter His presence through worship, prayer, Bible study, or fellowship, my heart is open to receive from Him. In that context, it is much more difficult for the devil to feed my mind with his words or thoughts.

Another truth we know about these "revelations" is that they are partial. The Bible makes it clear that the one who prophesies does so in part (see 1 Cor. 13:9). Because we have only partial knowledge, we can only impart partial revelation. In that same passage, we are even told that some prophecies will fail. In the Old Testament, no mistakes were allowed for the prophets, but that is not the teaching of the New Testament. I have heard Paul Cain say, "If some of your prophecies fail, then you know that you are a New Testament prophet."

It should be remembered that these "words" are also conditional; we must act. We cannot just sit back and wait for something to happen, but rather we are encouraged to use the words to wage war (see 1 Tim. 1:18). The enemy will attempt to sidetrack the plan of God, but when God's directives have been spoken, we can use that "word" as a weapon to bring the enemy down and assure the victory that God has in store for us. When a "word" is spoken, it is time to go to prayer. After we test that word, we can pray these exhortations and encouragements into reality.

A third truth that I like to tell people about the prophetic is that the "words" are in process. When a "word" comes to you, God will walk you through a process to bring it to pass. These partial and conditional words may take some time to be fulfilled. Once again, this is a good opportunity to seek the Lord for direction through prayer. We should be ready to enter into a time of intense seeking of the Lord to find His will and destiny for our lives.

God@Work

When a "word from the Lord" comes to a person, often there is an almost immediate interpretation. I have found through the years that the first interpretation is probably not the right one. If it was that easy to figure out, you didn't need this "insight" from the Lord. Usually I have found that, over time, a number of these insights from God begin to line up. You hear one this day, and another a few days later. After the first one they are not as much revelation as they are confirmation. And as they come, each one adds a little more to the whole, until you begin to receive a much clearer picture of what the Lord has for you.

I had all of those things in mind when I began to receive this impression for Dennis and Megan, and as Wilma and I waited upon the Lord through the night. The next morning the four of us sat in a quiet place where we could talk. Before I had spoken very long, it was obvious that Megan and Dennis had been considering the same things that I was about to tell them. Even though we did not know the Doyles well, we knew that they owned a successful business in Minneapolis. It was about the business that the Lord was speaking. As I recall, this is the essence of what I said:

"Dennis, I believe the Lord may be saying you are not to sell your business. You have been thinking about selling the business in order to 'go into the ministry.' But the Lord says you are already in the ministry. You are to keep your business, and you are to begin to see your business as your ministry. You are to treat your business as the flock of God, for He has called you as a steward over all those who work for you. In addition to those that work for you, God is going to open the door to minister to other CEOs about making their businesses into ministries as well."

The Doyles responded quickly to this word, and any thoughts of selling the business to enter the ministry were put aside. Their business would be their ministry. Throughout the intervening years, Wilma and I have become much closer to the Doyles, and have watched from a distance as God has done an amazing work through these two people. You have read what Megan has written in this book about the results of praying for the business, about leading a fully integrated life of faith and business, and about weekly prayer meetings for the business. You have seen both Megan's heart, and through her the heart of her husband as they have begun to walk into the "calling of ministry in business."

The Lord began to give me revelation about God's ongoing activity in the marketplace and in the lives of business and professional people. As this truth began to capture more and more of my attention, the day came when I realized I needed to put the material into book form. Over dinner one evening at our home in San Jose, the Doyles, Wilma, and I were talking about the book. Suddenly Wilma said, "Listen, this is very important." I knew by the sound of her voice that something very powerful was about to be spoken. She continued, "Rich, you are not to write the book alone. It would be a one-sided view. Megan is to write also, and you will have the viewpoint of the businessperson as well."

So, that which started one summer day a few years ago has continued to grow, and now we find ourselves immersed in this project. We sense a real urgency, because of the importance and timeliness of this issue.

I find as I travel around the world speaking and ministering to business leaders, that the message of this book is not new to most of them. But while it is not new, it is also a message that they have not often heard. How can this be true? The Lord has been speaking this message to many in the marketplace. They have heard it in their hearts, but they have not heard it preached or taught very often. However, a new day is dawning in which the Lord is releasing into the marketplace an army of soldiers who will be used as frontline ministers for the work of the Lord.

They are going to usher in a move of God unlike any we have seen. Some would refer to it as a revival, and while that may not be the best term, I will probably continue to use it simply for lack of a better one. There are many definitions for revival, but a very good and simple one is that of Richard and Kathryn Riss, "A revival is a sovereign move in which God pours out His Spirit upon all flesh."[5] This is what we are about to see: a sovereign move of God, not a revival in the traditional sense. It will not be something that takes place in a church or something that can be characterized by a series of meetings. An evangelist or a pastor will not spark this move of God, at least in the traditional understanding.

I am talking about that ongoing activity where God pours out His Spirit on all flesh. We are returning to the Biblical standard where we can expect to see God at work through the lives of business and professional people, CEOs and managers, policemen and nurses, athletes and salespeople. Yes, God is at work, and He wants to work through you!

I don't know how history will record it, and I am not even sure what to call it today. But I know this: God is actively working in the marketplace. In city after city, nation after nation, I find men and women to whom the Lord has been speaking. Without benefit of a sermon, a book, or a teaching tape, He has been imparting His revelation into the hearts of marketplace leaders. He is calling; He is stirring; He is anointing. Everywhere you look you see God at work.

It is time for the entire Body of Christ to learn how to work together to bring on the anointing of the Lord—kings and priests, working together so His "will be done on earth as it is in Heaven" (Luke 11:2b).

Endnotes

1. Jack Deere, *Surprised by the Power of the Spirit* (Grand Rapids, MI: Zondervan Publishing House, 1993), 214.

2. Max Lucado, *When God Whispers Your Name* (Dallas, TX: Word Publishing, 1994), 2.

3. Jack Deere, *Surprised by the Voice of God* (Grand Rapids, MI: Zondervan Publishing House, n.d.).

4. Cindy Jacobs, *The Voice of God* (Ventura, CA: Regal Books, n.d.).

5. Richard and Kathryn Riss, *Images of Revival: Another Wave Rolls In* (Shippensburg, PA: Revival Press, 1997), 1.

Rich Marshall is the president of ROI Ministries and vice president of Harvest Evangelism. He is also the concentration coordinator for Marketplace Ministries with the Wagner Leadership Institute, and is a founding member of Nehemiah Partners. You can receive information about product, scheduling and training opportunities by contacting Rich Marshall:

ROI Equipping
441 Camille Circle, Suite 11
San Jose, CA 95134
rich@springs.org
www.Godisworking.com

Additional copies of this book and other
book titles from Destiny Image are
available at your local bookstore.

For a complete list of our titles,
visit us at www.destinyimage.com
Send a request for a catalog to:

Destiny Image® Publishers, Inc.
P.O. Box 310
Shippensburg, PA 17257-0310

*"Speaking to the Purposes of God for This
Generation and for the Generations to Come"*